The Bloodiest Days

The Battles of 1861 and 1862

The Bloodiest Days

The Battles of 1861 and 1862

The House Divided
The Civil War

Corinne J. Naden & Rose Blue

RSVP

RAINTREE
STECK-VAUGHN
PUBLISHERS
A Steck-Vaughn Company

Austin, Texas

www.steck-vaughn.com

For Maire Plunkett Baldwin, my favorite college kid, with love, from Corinne
For my very good friend Sam Roth, with love, from Rose

Published by Raintree Steck-Vaughn Publishers,
an imprint of Steck-Vaughn Company

Publishing Director: Walter Kossmann
Editor: Shirley Shalit
Project Management & Design: Gino Coverty
Cover Design: Gino Coverty
Media Researcher: Claudette Landry
Electronic Production: Scott Melcer, Gino Coverty

Consultant: Paul Finkelman, University of Tulsa, College of Law

Library of Congress Cataloging-in-Publication Data

Naden, Corinne J.
   The bloodiest days: battles of 1861 and 1862 / Corinne J. Naden & Rose Blue.
      p.   cm. — (The house divided)
     Includes bibliographical references and index.
     Summary: Describes some of the most violent battles in the first two years of the Civil War, including the first and second battles at Bull Run, Shiloh, and Antietam.
    ISBN 0-8172-5581-8
     1. United States — History — Civil War, 1861-1865 — Campaigns Juvenile literature. [1. United States — History — Civil War, 1861-1865 — Campaigns.]
I. Blue, Rose. II. Title. III. Series: Naden, Corinne J. House divided.
E470.N34 1999
973.7'3 — dc21
                                                      99-15599
                                                    CIP   AC

Cover photo: The Battle of Antietam, September 17, 1862.

Title page photo: Battle of the *Monitor* and the *Merrimac* on March 9, 1862.

Acknowledgments listed on page 112 constitute part of this page.

Contents

The Glorious Adventure

Prologue

The American Civil War was the bloodiest in U.S. history. More Americans died in this war than any other. And in this bloodiest of wars, the first two years would see the bloodiest of days. Yet, strangely enough, the first battle of the Civil War did not produce a single battle death. On April 12, 1861, Confederate troops fired the first shots. The target was Fort Sumter, the Federal outpost in the harbor of Charleston, South Carolina.

But the Civil War really started because the North and the South never could agree about slavery and states' rights. For years, a mostly verbal, but highly passionate, battle had been waged in and out of Congress. The North was antislavery. At the very least, it did not want slavery extended into new territories. The South was equally determined. It not only wanted slavery, it wanted Federal protection for the institution and against slave rebellions. And it wanted Federal enforcement of the fugitive slave law in the Compromise of 1850, to guarantee return of runaway slaves to their owners.

An uneasy truce existed for years. Both sides more or less "agreed to disagree." Then, in November 1860, Republican Abraham Lincoln of Illinois was elected President of the United States—without a single electoral vote from the South. It wasn't so much his attitude about slavery. Lincoln was considered a moderate. He personally was against what some called a "peculiar institution," but recognized the right of the South to own slaves. Lincoln and the Republicans, however, were firmly against the spread of slavery beyond its present boundaries. That meant into new territories or states. The South could see the future. As new nonslaveholding states entered the Union, the slave states would soon be far outnumbered. As early as 1858, Lincoln had declared his belief that the nation could not permanently exist half slave, half free. It would have to be one or the other.

With Lincoln in the White House, the South saw the end of its way of life. So, some six weeks after his election, South Carolina seceded from the United States. By February 1, 1861, Mississippi, Florida, Alabama, Georgia, Louisiana, and Texas had followed. Three days later, these seven became the Confederate States of America, with Jefferson Davis of Mississippi as president.

On Inauguration Day, March 4, 1861, Lincoln urged the seceding states to return. But it was too late for cooler heads to listen. Fort Sumter was attacked in April, and the precious union that had become the United States of America was broken.

The almost bloodless takeover in Charleston Harbor began the bloodiest war in U.S. history. President Lincoln reacted quickly. He called for 75,000 volunteers to put down this rebellion. Since the United States did not recognize the right of the Confederates to secede, the Civil War was, technically, a rebellion.

The President's request got him volunteers—and more trouble. Eight slave states were still in the Union. Would they stay at the price of firing on their Confederate neighbors? No, said Virginia,

This 1860 notice in a South Carolina newspaper combines pro-secession feeling with a little sly advertising.

Cotton plantations, as in this idealized picture, were symbolic of what was thought to be the Southern way of life.

Arkansas, and North Carolina. No, said Tennessee, the last state to join the Confederacy, on June 8, 1861. Eleven states had now seceded. The border slave states of Kentucky, Missouri, Maryland, and Delaware cautiously decided to remain with the Union.

The sides were drawn. The guns were loaded. Emotions reached fever pitch. "Get the Johnny Rebs!" screamed the Northerners. "The Union troops are yankee doodles," yelled the Southerners. "How dare you insult the Stars and Stripes!" "Preserve the Southern way of life!" Patriotism washed over the North and South. Men flocked to recruiting stations in their haste to join. Women took up sewing needles and threw themselves into the war effort. There are many colorful, strange, exciting, and tragic stories of those who participated in this experience. It was a wild, emotional, patriotic time.

But this is a book that focuses on the battlefield during the war's bloodiest days. Both sides were dedicated to preserving the right as they saw it. Both sides, however, were woefully unprepared for war.

No war statistics are ever 100 percent accurate, and this is certainly true of the Civil War. Record keeping was not a science, and most sources disagree to some extent on casualty, death, and other figures. However, generally speaking, about three million men fought in the Civil War on both sides and more than 600,000 died. The United States lost about 360,000 men in battle, or from mortal wounds, disease, prison camps, and other causes. These include about 5,000 sailors. The Confederate States' losses numbered about 258,000 from all causes. However, strange as it sounds, soldiers were safer on the battlefield than off it! They were far more likely to die of poor medical care or disease such as typhoid, malaria, smallpox, pneumonia, and even measles.

Dead soldiers after the Battle of Antietam– a tragic scene repeated over and over during the Civil War.

One of the reasons the Civil War is referred to as "the bloodiest war" is that the casualties in a single engagement were so often staggering. In the two-day battle for Shiloh, the North's number of dead, wounded, and missing totaled more than 13,000 men, nearly 11,000 for the South. In a single day at Antietam, the figures were 12,000 for the North, perhaps as many as 13,000 for the South. It was not unusual for entire regiments to be nearly wiped out. At the Battle of Gettysburg, for instance, the Twenty-Sixth North Carolina regiment lost, from death, wounds, or missing, 708 men out of a total of 880!

This very young soldier, Austin Johnson of the 16th Massacussetts Infantry, was killed at the Battle of Gettysburg.

At first glance, it would seem that the South had no chance at all against the far larger North. There were 23 states left in the Union at the start of the war, with about 21 million people. The South had 11 states and a population of about 9 million, of which more than one-third were slaves. The North had about 100,000 manufacturing plants, the South about 18,000. The North had 70 percent of the railroads and a navy of 90 ships. The South had no navy at all.

What the South did have, however, was the advantage of fighting mostly on its own turf, defending its own homeland. In war, it is generally an advantage to be the defender rather than the attacker. For one thing, the South's supply and communication lines would be shorter than that of the invading North. Historians generally think that the two sides were fairly evenly matched as long as the South fought a defensive war. It might, therefore, be said that had the Confederacy done a better job politically and economically, it might indeed have won the war!

The South did lack the manufacturing power of the North, but the Confederates expected both France and England to favor their side, if only to keep the steady supply of Southern cotton going to Europe. Unfortunately for the South, that did not happen.

Another advantage for the South was its military leadership. Both sides had able officers who had been trained at the U.S. Military Academy at West Point, but of the eight military colleges in the United States at the time, seven were in the South. One of these alone provided the Confederacy with 1,781 officers.

Of the soldiers themselves, both sides were similar. The vast majority were volunteers. They were generally young, most in their early to mid twenties, although some were far younger. According to records, 127 soldiers in the Union army were just 13 years old! Whatever their age or experience, they tended to grow up in a hurry.

A word must be said about the "other" fighting men in the Civil War. Besides Yankee Doodle and Johnny Reb, thousands of American blacks, known then as Negroes or coloreds, fought and died for the cause of the North and for freedom. About 186,000 blacks joined the Union army and some 32,000 died. Another 50,000 served as noncombatant laborers, and about 18,000 were in the U.S. Navy. Twenty-one received the newly created Medal of Honor, the country's highest award.

Black soldiers faced not only the threat of death in battle, but the prejudices of their fellow soldiers. White Northerners may have been against slavery, but they were rarely for fighting side by side with a black man. It was not until late 1862 that Congress, facing a shortage of troops, allowed full-scale recruitment of black soldiers. Although not often accepted as equals, black troops

These Union soldiers, stationed at Fort Corcoran, are part of the 107th Colored Infantry assigned to protect the capital, Washington, D.C.

slowly began to earn respect simply because of their performance in battle. They fought in more than 33 major engagements. Wrote Major General James G. Blunt, a white soldier, of his 1st Kansas Colored Volunteers, "Their coolness and bravery I have never seen surpassed."

Blacks were in the Confederate army, too. Some slaves and free men became cooks or servants or musicians. A few even stood guard duty, although Southerners were generally fearful of "arming slaves," or accepting them as soldiers, which would imply a kind of equality. Desperately needing recruits, the Confederacy did pass a law in early 1865 allowing enlistment of black soldiers. The war ended before any of them saw combat.

Large groups of foreign-born volunteers fought for the Blue and Gray—Germans, Canadians, the English and Irish, for example. Several thousand Native Americans also fought on each side; some were ill treated or else ignored by their white comrades. But many became respected soldiers and admired heroes. Stand Watie, a Cherokee leader and Confederate general, raised a regiment of Cherokee mounted riflemen. He was one of the last Confederate generals to surrender, on June 23, 1865.

Probably the most unique of "fighting men" for both North and South were the "women." Perhaps as many as a few hundred women disguised themselves as men and joined the army. In some cases, their secret wasn't discovered for months. For Jennie Hodgers, it took years! She joined the 95th Illinois Volunteers as Albert Cashier and fought at Vicksburg and Nashville. Her fellow soldiers described her as "the smallest man in the company." She collected a military pension after the war and

Not all Civil War soldiers were men or boys. This disguised woman was a member of the Union Zouave troops. The colorful uniform was copied from that of the original French-Algerian infantry.

pension board threatened to stop her payments, her old war buddies testified on her behalf. Jennie, alias Albert, kept her pension.

Most everyone is familiar with some battle names from the Civil War, places such as Gettysburg or Shiloh or Missionary Ridge. Books such as this one talk about these places because they were the scenes of much life and death drama and because it was mainly on those battlefields that the war was won and lost. But it should be remembered that many Americans on both sides gave their lives in small, largely unheard-of sites with names such as Ball's Bluff, Virginia, or Brice's Cross Roads, Mississippi.

Besides names of towns or battle sites, the armies themselves are often called by many names. Here, we refer to the United States of America as the North, Federals, or the Union, sometimes the Blue, or even the slang Yankees. The South may be the Confederacy or Confederates, the Gray, or even the Rebels.

This war that was fought between 1861 and 1865 also has been called, rightly or wrongly, by many names—the U.S. or American Civil War, the War for the Union, the War for Southern Independence, even the War Between the States. Some call it a war of liberation, which freed four million slaves. Some speak of it as a family war, because, especially in the border states, some families had soldiers in both armies. There are even a few tales of a soldier capturing or killing one of his relatives. But the vast majority of soldiers fought side by side with friends, neighbors, and family members. The official name of the Civil War, however, is the War of the Rebellion.

In the spirited patriotism of the moment, many young men on both sides willingly went off to war as though in a sacred test of honor and courage. The first of them fell in July 1861, near a sluggish little stream in northern Virginia. It was called Bull Run, a not-so-glamorous site to begin this "glorious adventure."

First Battle:

First Bull Run
July 21, 1861

The United States of America was now at war with the 11 seceding states of the Confederacy. Led by President Jefferson Davis, the South felt justified in its cause and confident of its ability to defend its homeland. U.S. President Abraham Lincoln had just taken over a government that was ill prepared for war. His predecessor, President James Buchanan, had spent too long trying to compromise. Yet, Lincoln called for 75,000 troops to serve only a three-month period, an indication of how short he thought the war would be.

An artist's version of the chaos, terror, and bravery at the First Battle of Bull Run.

Fort Sumter was lost. Now it was time for the first major battle.

The South calls it First Manassas. The North says it's the First Battle of Bull Run. Can't these two even agree on where they were? Actually, they do. But Southerners often named a battle after the nearest town; in this case, Manassas. Northerners generally chose the nearest piece of geography; in this case, Bull Run, a stream which meanders slowly near the town of Manassas, located about 40 miles southwest of Washington, D.C.

Whatever they called it, the bloody fight was a shock to both sides. The South won, but many of the young soldiers, Blue and Gray, were so traumatized by the horror of their first battle that they ran from it. But that wasn't the shocking part. Nearly 5,000 soldiers, North and South, died or were wounded or captured in this first major battle of the Civil War. And all that carnage took just one single day! That was a shock. So was the sight of the peaceful Virginia countryside covered with bodies of the dead and dying.

The North and the South learned a powerful lesson on that one day in July. They learned that there is absolutely nothing romantic about war. And the sharpest military minds on both sides learned that this particular war was going to be long and terrible.

The main problem with Bull Run was that no one was ready to fight it. It's a wonder that anyone won. The dapper Confederate General P.G.T.—for Pierre Gustave Toutant—Beauregard was hailed as a great leader after First Manassas. But

BRIGADIER GENERAL IRVIN McDOWELL

Brigadier General Irvin McDowell (1818–1885), a West Point graduate, had served through the Mexican War. He would also fight at Second Bull Run in 1862. Criticized for his conduct, he never held another command during the Civil War.

Beauregard was a flashy sort and his military plans tended to be on the elaborate side. He spent much of the time before this battle trying to decide whether to attack the enemy or defend the area. Orders from Richmond finally ordered him to defend.

The South was lucky that the Union leaders proved even more incompetent, even though Brigadier General Irvin McDowell drew up a sound plan of attack. He had been appointed commander of the Department of Northeastern Virginia just two months earlier. But Union leadership at Bull Run was a mess. Every order seemed to be the wrong one. Every movement turned out a failure. And in the true tradition of the military, McDowell took the blame for it all.

The South may have needed a little luck to win, but not so lucky were all those who died or were wounded at Bull Run. The North's casualties were more than 600 dead, 950 wounded, and about 1,200 captured. The victorious South wasn't in much better shape. About 600 died in battle or later of their wounds and another 1,375 were wounded but lived. (There are no figures for the number of Confederate soldiers who were captured.) All this happened on July 21, 1861, along a small, winding ribbon of water that many of those in the fight hadn't even heard of a few days before.

For just plain battlefield drama, however, Bull Run had a lot going for it—whatever it was called. In that battle, one of the South's most able generals

OH, THE GLORY OF BATTLE!

"I must join the boys from Illinois!" shouted Congressman John A. Logan. He was attending a formal party when he heard about the coming fight. Immediately, he left Washington for the Virginia countryside. But Illinois had no unit at Bull Run. That stopped Logan only for a moment. He walked right on the battlefield and joined a Michigan regiment. Congressman Logan may have been the first American to go to war wearing top hat and tails.

earned his legendary nickname—Thomas Jonathan "Stonewall" Jackson. The Battle of Bull Run was also dramatic because it marked the beginning of the end of American innocence. It seems strange today, but in the mid-nineteenth century, many, perhaps most, Americans looked upon the upcoming civil war as a kind of high-spirited, exciting adventure.

Civilians from nearby Washington, D.C.—ladies in their finest bonnets and gentlemen carrying festively packed picnic baskets—set out for northern Virginia for the grand spectacle. They planned on spreading their blankets and sipping their wine, and by the end of act one, the show would surely be over. The superior Northern army would have routed the upstart rebels.

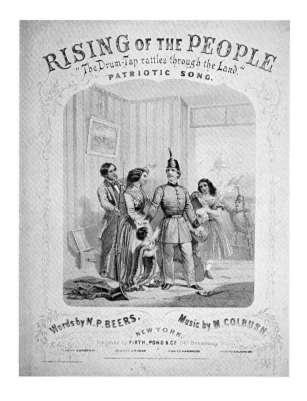

A sentimental print decorates the cover of a piece of patriotic sheet music that sold for 50 cents a copy. The theme of brave women sending their brothers and husbands off to battle was a popular one on both sides as war began.

Not quite. What the spectators actually saw were green fields turned red with the blood of the dead and dying. What they heard were cries of agony from the wounded who lay largely unattended in the misery all around them. Suddenly, war didn't seem quite so glamorous.

Average Americans of another century were perhaps more trusting of government than Americans are today. They believed almost without question in the ideals they had been taught at home and in school. War was a time for a brave young man in his handsome uniform to go "a-soldiering." It was a time for a young woman to weep and sew a handkerchief for her beloved to keep him safe in battle. It was a time to "save the Union," or "preserve the Southern way of life."

There was no television news, no radio broadcasts during the Civil War to show Americans how horrible war could be. Although many newspapers and photographers, especially in the North, reported on the war, there were no instant pictures of dead men and horses that covered the fields as far as one could see. The young men of both sides who got their first taste of war at Bull Run were paralyzed by the ferocious sound of the guns. A Northern officer said later that after the first shots, his men just stood with their mouths open, staring, obeying not one single order. One entire Confederate regiment was so traumatized by the sight of men falling around them that they just walked off the battlefield and picked blackberries.

First Bull Run may have shown soldier and civilian alike how terrible war was, but it did more than that. It made both sides more determined than ever to win. Somehow that would atone for all those who had died. The American Civil War was going to be a long, long struggle.

Totally dedicated to the Southern cause, President Jefferson Davis proved to be an aloof, often difficult leader.

Why did the first big battle of the war take place at Bull Run? The answer is Manassas. It may have been just a sleepy little southern town, but it was also a railroad junction. Rail lines from the Shenandoah Valley to the west met lines from Alexandria to the east, and they crossed with lines that ran south to the Confederate capital of Richmond. Anyone who controlled the rail lines controlled transportation in northern Virginia. And transportation in the 1860s meant the railroad. And the railroad meant moving troops and equipment and supplies. The side that controlled the rail lines was bound to win the war.

President Abraham Lincoln knew that. So did the Confederate president, Jefferson Davis. And so did all the Northern and Southern military leaders. Of course, actually getting it done was another matter entirely.

The North wasn't ready for a major fight in mid–1861. Neither was the South. Troops on both sides were eager but overwhelmingly untrained. Even so, Northerners were upset about Confederate troops in Virginia so near to Washington, D.C. President Lincoln was getting pressured from all sides to do something! What he really wanted to do was wait. Wait for more soldiers to be recruited and trained. Wait for the plan favored by General of the Army Winfield Scott to take effect. Scott wanted to blockade the Atlantic seacoast, control traffic on the Mississippi, and starve the Confederates into giving up. Given the North's superior navy and larger army, it might have worked. It certainly would have been less bloody. It also would have taken a lot of time. That's what Lincoln didn't have.

In June, word reached the President that the North had lost a battle at Big Bethel in southern Virginia. That seemed to open a corridor for Confederate troops to march straight up to Washington. Suddenly, Lincoln didn't have any time left at all. He had to do something. So acting immediately he ordered General

A QUESTION OF LOYALTY

General of the Army Winfield Scott (1786–1866) was a Virginian. So, it was only natural to ask about his loyalty when war came. His reply? "I have served my country, under the flag of the Union, for more than 50 years. I will defend that flag with my sword, even if my native State assails it." A dashing young officer in the War of 1812, Scott had grown a bit heavier over the years. He stood six foot five and weighed about 300 pounds. He walked with difficulty and at age 74, the general was older than the Constitution of his country. But his mind was still brilliant and his heart still loyal.

Scott to mount a campaign—ready or not—in northern Virginia.

Scott delegated the Bull Run job to Brigadier General Irvin McDowell of Ohio. Although his experience qualified him, McDowell was not pleased. He complained that his troops were too few and too green. Scott told him the South had just as many inexperienced troops. In other words, get on with it.

General McDowell was 42 years old, a veteran of the Mexican War, and a poor leader. Often rude and prone to temper tantrums, he constantly forgot the names and faces of his subordinate officers. He did not inspire confidence in his men, and they tended to stay away from him. But he was not stupid and was, in fact, a good planner. His attack strategy for Bull Run was quite sound.

McDowell's plan divided his Federal army into three columns. They would all march west on roughly parallel routes. One column would march on Fairfax Court House, 16 miles from Washington, and capture the Southern posts there. It would join a second column and mount a diversionary attack on the Confederate line at Bull Run. The third Union column—the important one in the plan—would strike to the south, cutting off the rail lines to Richmond.

Naturally, the South knew the North was going to attack. The Union army had made no secret of its plans. Probably half the country knew about it. But when? That problem was solved on July 10 when a young woman named Bettie Duval was shown into the tent of Confederate Brigadier General Milledge L. Bonham. A spy for the South, she removed from her mass of dark hair, a note saying that McDowell's army would move on July 16. And so it did. Beauregard ordered his troops to spread out in a meandering eight-mile-line that was strung along the riverbanks of the Bull Run.

So it was that on Sunday morning, July 21, 1861, a Federal army of about 35,000 men with less than adequate training was preparing to do battle. So was a Confederate force of just about the same size and just about as inexperienced.

General Beauregard, in overall command of the Southern troops, was ordered by General Robert E. Lee only to defend Bull Run, but not to launch an attack. Reinforcements were on the way. Beauregard decided the best defensive position was south of the river with its five-foot-high banks and only one bridge, on the Warrenton Turnpike, where army wagons could cross. But an army could walk across the sluggish stream at several places, so Beauregard had to spread his men thin.

THE LADIES ARE FOR SPYING

Bettie Duval was one of many young Virginia ladies who were eager to serve the South and did so by charming their way through unsuspecting Yankee lines to get information about troop movements. All this smacked of high melodrama and pure fiction, but it was repeated again and again throughout the war. And although many items that the young women brought into Southern camps from Washington proved to be worthless, Duval's message was not.

Belle Boyd, one of a number of Southern women who aided the war effort by spying for the Confederacy.

GENERAL P.G.T. BEAUREGARD

General P.G.T. Beauregard (1818–1893) declared without the slightest trace of modesty, "My soldiers have the most unbounded confidence in me." This Louisiana-born West Point soldier, although a capable commander, was inclined to be rather impressed with his own importance. When ordered not to attack, the dapper officer wrung his hands and bemoaned his inability to defend Bull Run. "Oh, that I had the genius of a Napoleon," he declared before the battle. Most of those around him felt that Beauregard already believed he had that quality.

Although a dandy and a bit of a braggart, nonetheless General P.G.T. Beauregard acquitted himself well in battle.

Rebel troops stretched out along Bull Run for five miles … waiting.

At first it seemed as though the showy Beauregard was a poor choice. His orders to his men were often confusing or poorly considered. He ordered certain positions to be defended by a number of brigades but didn't say which ones. He sent several brigades to defend the same site along Bull Run, leaving other locations unprotected.

Things didn't look much better for the Union. McDowell had spent the night before the battle in his tent with a stomachache. Most of his men couldn't sleep either. Many of them wrote their last-ever letters home in the predawn hours.

The North moved first on the morning of the battle. McDowell sent his men across the creek a little after nine. The Rebels waited. But the North had trouble from the very beginning. McDowell had no good maps of the territory, so his soldiers had to stay on the narrow dirt roads, which slowed the march to a crawl. Each hour grew hotter and more dusty, made worse by the heavy woolen uniforms that the troops—on both sides—wore. The men sang songs and sometimes stopped to catch

SAYING GOOD-BYE

"I have no misgivings about, or lack of confidence in the cause in which I am engaged, and my courage does not halt or falter," wrote Major Sullivan Ballou to his wife in Rhode Island. He spoke of the thousands of men sleeping around him on this calm summer night and of his suspicion that death was lurking near. Assuring his wife and children of his constant devotion, the 32-year-old lawyer described his love of country in this way: "I know how strongly American Civilization now leans on the triumph of the Government, and

how great a debt we owe to those who went before us..." He added, "If it is necessary that I should fall on the battle field for my Country, I am ready." We can't, of course, know if the major was truly ready, but he did die at the Battle of Bull Run on July 21, 1861.

chickens or pick berries, despite their officers' best efforts to maintain some kind of control.

Without adequate maps or even scouting reports, Yankee soldiers stumbled about with no idea of where they were or where they were going. And McDowell proved himself inept as well. Instead of telling the brigade that was farthest from Bull Run to move in first so that all brigades would meet at the stream at the same time, he moved the nearest brigade first. It took him an hour to realize his mistake.

Even so, and despite the blunders, McDowell began to look

A Confederate woman makes sure her husband's uniform is correct to the last detail before he goes off to war. The sunguard she is adjusting was rarely used.

SOMETIMES LEADERSHIP FALTERS

Brigadier General Samuel P. Heintzelman, a hero of the Mexican War, commanded the southernmost Union column at Bull Run. But his mind seems to have been elsewhere when his entire force came to a standstill because the soldiers had to walk in single file on a narrow bridge across the stream. The whole march was held up for hours. Heintzelman might have missed the battle entirely except for one of his officers who showed a little take-charge ability. Colonel Oliver O. Howard of Maine just got tired of waiting and told his men to walk through the water. Bull Run, it turned out, was only knee deep.

Howard, who would rise to major general and lose an arm in battle, became one of the great heroes of the war. Howard University in Washington, D.C., is named for him.

like a genius for a while that Sunday morning. His men tore into the Confederates, driving them from one position to another. Some of the Northern boys reacted with glee. "The war is over!" they shouted. There were great cries of encouragement to General McDowell as he rode back and forth among the troops, his dress uniform and white gloves splendid in the morning sun.

A short time later, however, things didn't look quite so splendid. Beauregard's reinforcements—General Joseph E. Johnston and his brigades from the Shenandoah Valley, General Thomas J. Jackson and his Virginians, and Brigadier General Barnard E. Bee, a distinguished veteran from South Carolina, with volunteers from many Southern states—arrived on the Manassas railroad. Johnston was actually the senior general at Bull Run, but because Beauregard knew the territory better, he was left in command.

Northern and Southern armies finally clashed in a frenzy of mayhem and killing that surprised everyone. Colonel William Tecumseh Sherman and his 2nd Wisconsin had crossed Bull Run

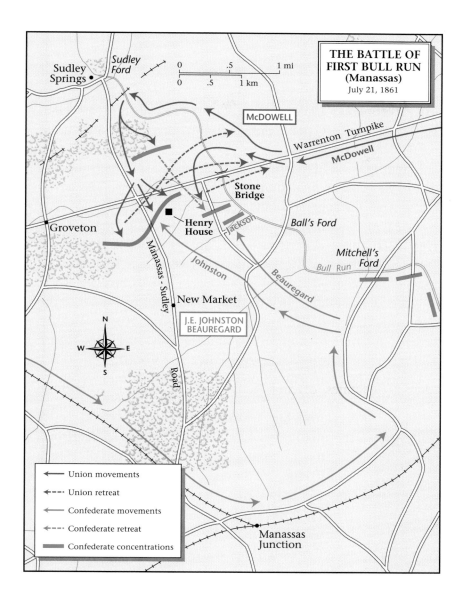

THE BATTLE OF FIRST BULL RUN
(Manassas)
July 21, 1861

Sudley Springs •

Sudley Ford

McDOWELL

0   .5   1 mi
0   .5   1 km

Warrenton Turnpike

McDowell

Stone Bridge

Groveton

Henry House

Jackson

Ball's Ford

Mitchell's Ford

Bull Run

Johnston

Beauregard

New Market

Manassas - Sudley

J.E. JOHNSTON
BEAUREGARD

N
W   E
S

Road

⟵ Union movements
⟵--- Union retreat
⟵ Confederate movements
⟵--- Confederate retreat
▬▬ Confederate concentrations

Manassas Junction

The first major conflict between the armies of the United States and the Confederacy took place only 25 miles from Washington, D.C., and began in an almost picnic-like atmosphere.

stream Since their brigade uniforms were gray instead of the Federal blue, their advance was not detected at first. (At this point in the war, some uniform colors could vary and cause confusion.) But soon the Rebels were fleeing. Despite all the setbacks and mistakes, McDowell now had only to get his men three miles down the road to reach the precious railroad. Then he could cut off the Confederate troops from any more reinforcements.

Standing up in his stirrups, a jubilant McDowell raced up and down the lines of men shouting, "Victory! Victory! The day is ours!" Alas, the general shouted too soon.

By 2 p.m., Union troops were ready to march up Henry House Hill to complete the victory. But, on the other side, General Jackson, without waiting for orders, had been marching his men toward the hill as well, arriving in the area shortly before noon.

Then Jackson did a curious thing. Instead of rushing into the fight that General Bee was currently losing nearby, Jackson ordered his men to stop just behind the crest of Henry House Hill. There they formed a defensive line and waited.

General Jackson was known for his sometimes eccentric decisions, and no one knows exactly why he took such a stand.

One of the Civil War's most famous war heroes, Confederate General Thomas J. "Stonewall" Jackson.

Certainly Bee, whose troops were in retreat under thunderous Union guns, didn't know. As the Rebels began scrambling back over the crest of Henry House Hill, Bee dashed up to Jackson on his horse and shouted, "General, they are beating us back!" A calm Jackson replied, "Sir, we'll give them the bayonet." That seemed to reassure Bee that Jackson would back him up, and he galloped off to spur his battle-weary men into one more stand.

It was said later that as Bee approached his troops, he pointed back toward the brigade of Virginians and said something to the effect that "Jackson is standing there like a stone wall." In that manner, the eccentric commander from Virginia became, for all time, General Stonewall Jackson.

When it seemed that surely the South would be

defeated, General McDowell had to reorganize his troops for the final surge. In that time, Generals Johnston and Beauregard rallied their own men. They prepared to take a stand. Beauregard had so recovered his composure that he rode up and down among his weary soldiers, telling them to hang on just a little longer. At one point, his horse was shot out from under him, but he calmly picked himself up and mounted another horse.

Over the next few hours, a terrible battle waged, with one side gaining advantage only to be pushed back. Although both sides fought bravely, McDowell kept sending one brigade at a time against the Confederates, instead of overwhelming them with superior numbers. The mistake proved fatal. In the late afternoon, the North sent its last brigades into the melee—three from Maine and one from Vermont.

Beauregard seized this moment to send his entire line to the attack. Confusion reigned. In desperate panic, the Union lines began to break. By 4:30, the retreat was on. Crazed men ran for their lives. The Northern forces were out of control.

So tired were the Confederates that Beauregard stopped their pursuit of the fleeing Federals. The battle was over. The South

STONEWALL!

Thirty-seven-year-old Thomas Jonathan Jackson (1824–1863), West Point graduate from the state of Virginia, came to the battle of Bull Run with a largely unremarkable career. He left it with an admiring nickname and a place in the history books. He was a skillful strategist, a stern disciplinarian, and a leader of unquestioned bravery. He could keep his head under fire. Some sources, however, have questioned just how Jackson earned his famous nickname of "Stonewall." They speculate that perhaps Bee was not being exactly complimentary when he said, "There is Jackson standing like a stone wall." Another officer on the scene later said that Bee was actually furious at Jackson for standing "like a stone wall" and not coming to his aid. Was Bee really insulting Jackson? We'll never really know, of course, and it really makes no difference. Stonewall Jackson he is, no matter what General Bee said... or meant. And the battle had turned.

General Irvin McDowell (fifth from right) and his staff on the steps of Robert E. Lee's Arlington, Virginia, home. Lee's home had been seized by the Union forces.

had won. Once again, General P.G.T. Beauregard was a hero.

But poor General McDowell. Deserved or not, he goes down in history as the leader of not only a losing battle but a disgraceful retreat. The North was humiliated as demoralized soldiers, dirty and hungry, trudged back into the nation's capital. Yet McDowell should not take all the blame for the disaster. In fact, as General Sherman said, McDowell had organized "one of the best-planned battles of the war." His orders and plans were better thought out than were Beauregard's, but they were simply too sophisticated for green recruits, who had no battle experience. Also, McDowell did not gather enough information about roads in the area to move his troops. He did not send a strong enough force of soldiers into battle at the same time. Of course, he didn't really want a major battle at all. He just wanted to push past the Rebels and cut them off from Richmond. But when he saw that a major battle was indeed taking place, he should have changed his plans. He did not. So, McDowell takes the blame.

Fellow officers didn't want to blame McDowell, but the public and press certainly didn't mind. Many labeled him a drunk and also chastised every general in the entire Federal army for the loss. Saner heads found new resolve in the defeat. National honor must be avenged.

But how could the demoralized Union army win back its pride? Lincoln figured it better be without McDowell. So, Scott called in General George B. McClellan to command what would become the Army of the Potomac. McClellan became a hero for the Union, until later in the war when he, too, was criticized and replaced.

Both sides buried their dead along Bull Run, and the grass grew green once more. The town of Manassas went back to being sleepy. In a year, the armies would return.

Abraham Lincoln reacted to the disaster in characteristic silence. But when a congressman chanced to ask him about any news of the battle, good or bad, the President whispered, "It's damned bad." And, for the Union, indeed it was.

AN IRRETRIEVABLE MISFORTUNE

Edwin M. Stanton (1814–1869), soon to be named Lincoln's secretary of war, was horrified by the outcome at Bull Run. He wrote to former President James Buchanan, on July 26, 1861: "The dreadful disaster of Sunday can scarcely be mentioned. The imbecility of this Administration culminated in that catastrophe—an irretrievable misfortune and national disgrace never to be forgotten are to be added to the ruin of all peaceful pursuits and national bankruptcy as the result of Lincoln's 'running the machine' for five months.... The capture of Washington seems now to be inevitable."

Edward Stanton became Lincoln's secretary of war in January 1862.

THE BATTLE OF THE MIGHTY IRONCLADS

The Battle of the Mighty Ironclads, as viewed by Lieutenant William F. Keeler, paymaster on the *Monitor*: "As a light fog lifted from the water it revealed the *Merrimac* with her consorts lying under Sewall's Point. The announcement of breakfast brought also the news that the *Merrimac* was coming, and our coffee was forgotten... A puff of smoke arose from her side and a shell howled over our heads... I experienced a peculiar sensation; I do not think it was fear, but it was different from anything I ever knew before. We were enclosed in what we supposed to be an impenetrable armor—we knew that a powerful foe was about to meet us—ours was an untried experiment and our enemy's first fire might make it a coffin for us all."

The battle of the Monitor *and the* Merrimac *in an 1892 painting.*

Then, the navy was back in the news, this time at Hampton Roads, Virginia, at the mouth of the James River. On the morning of March 9, 1862, the Union ship U.S.S. *Monitor* battled the Confederate's C.S.S. *Merrimac* (taken from the Norfolk naval shipyard by the South and renamed *Virginia*). This first duel between ironclad warships was a five-hour draw, but it signaled the end of wooden ships and the beginning of the modern age of naval warfare. Two months later, the Confederates would destroy the *Virginia* when they had to get out of Norfolk, and the *Monitor* was lost in a storm off North Carolina at the end of the same year.

But now it was springtime. Peach trees burst with delicate color along the Tennessee River in the southwestern part of the state. General Albert Sidney Johnston, with some 40,000 Confederate troops, was moving north. He was looking for General Grant.

Grant and his 42,000 men were camped on the west side of the Tennessee, at Pittsburg Landing. They had occupied the tiny port for about a month. Grant had been joined by a 42-year-old West

Federal sailors, both black and white, are entertained on board the ironclad Hunchback *in 1862.*

JOHNSTON AND GRANT, COMMANDERS AT SHILOH

The loss of Albert Sidney Johnston (1803–1862) at Shiloh was a terrible blow to the Confederate cause. Born in Kentucky and a West Point graduate (1826), he was appointed the second ranking general of the Confederate army by Jefferson Davis. His surprise attack on Union troops at Shiloh was almost successful.

Ulysses S. Grant (1822–1885), Ohio-born and the 18th president of the United States (1869–1877), had an up-and-down military career during the early years of the Civil War. Regarded as a heavy drinker, he was criticized for the great loss of life incurred during the Battle of Shiloh. By 1864, however, he would be given command over all the armies of the United States and would eventually bring about the surrender of General Robert E. Lee and the Confederate army at Appomattox Court House, April 9, 1865. His compassion and dignity in victory earned him high praise.

Generals Albert Sidney Johnston (top left) and Ulysses S. Grant.

Pointer and now brigadier general. This red-haired, brilliant, eccentric, and sometimes intensely nervous man was William Tecumseh Sherman. A commander in the disaster at First Bull Run, he had later suffered a nervous breakdown. Relieved of his duties, Sherman had rested for three months and had just returned to the army. Although he was superior in rank to Grant, he had taken a secondary position during this campaign, which Grant greatly appreciated. The two men would form a lifelong friendship.

Grant was waiting at Pittsburg Landing for General Don Carlos Buell and his 20,000-man Army of the Ohio. Once united, the Federals planned to attack the Confederate-held town of Corinth, about 22 miles to the south, just over the border in Mississippi.

Confederate General Johnston reasoned, quite rightly, that it might be a good idea to attack Grant before Buell's men arrived. However, his second in command, the dapper Beauregard of Sumter and Bull Run fame, was worried. Suppose Grant heard them coming? Suppose Buell's men had already arrived? The handsome and able Johnston seemed unconcerned. "I would fight them if they were a million," he said.

Beauregard needn't have fretted. Although Pittsburg Landing was easy to defend, the Federal army acted as though an attack was the last thing to expect. And, in fact, General Grant did not believe an attack was coming. Neither did Sherman. Incredibly, the day before the battle, these two experienced military leaders

General William Tecumseh Sherman

"WAR IS HELL"

William Tecumseh Sherman (1820–1891) was born in Ohio and graduated from West Point in 1840. After fighting at First Bull Run, Shiloh, and Vicksburg, he commanded the Army of the Tennessee and began his marches through Georgia. In the fall of 1864, he invaded the city of Atlanta and soon after, departed on his famous "march to the sea." The aim was to capture the city of Savannah, which Sherman did that December. But he left behind an Atlanta nearly destroyed by fire, although Sherman had meant only to burn military facilities. He earned for himself the everlasting hatred of Southern whites because he systematically destroyed the physical ability of the South to make war. When Grant became president in 1869, Sherman was named commanding general of the army, a post he held until 1884. He died in New York City. General Sherman is often quoted as the author of the phrase, "War is hell."

had no idea that an enemy force just about the size of their own stood off in the darkness, waiting. The Union army had dug no protective trenches. Grant had little use for trenches anyway, as did many West Pointers of the time. Nor had he stationed many lookouts around the area, even though it was heavily forested and, therefore, well suited to conceal advancing troops. Cavalry patrols, which might have given warnings, were not sent out on a regular basis. Picket lines around the area were casual. Also, the newest divisions, with the least fighting experience, to arrive at Pittsburg Landing were stationed so that they would be the first to be hit by the enemy.

Strange as it may seem, even when the Confederates were sighted, they were ignored! The day before the battle, Sherman was told that Rebel infantry had been spotted nearby. Sherman replied, "You militia officers get scared too easily." That afternoon, an elderly and very nervous commander from Ohio, Jesse J. Appler, was fired on while drilling his men some distance from the encampment. For suggesting that he was being attacked, Appler was laughed at because "there is no enemy nearer than Corinth." Accordingly, Appler's men stopped their war games and went back to hunting for wild onions.

It wasn't that the Northern troops were so naive, although most of them, indeed, had little knowledge of military planning. It wasn't that Grant was a poor commander, although he did make some errors of judgment. It was more that perhaps he had, not too little, but too much confidence. He simply believed his Union army to be invincible. Unfortunately for many, it was not.

And so came a beautiful day in spring, April 6, 1862. The peacefulness of a Sunday morning was blasted by the terrifying sight and sound of thousands upon thousands of Confederate soldiers rushing into the encampment. The Union men scarcely had time to grab their weapons.

Thus began one of the fiercest battles of the Civil War. Amid the bursting peach blossoms, fighting swirled around a little whitewashed Methodist church called Shiloh (pronounced shy - low). The name in Hebrew means "place of peace."

General Johnston could not believe his luck. Not only was his advance unnoticed, but Grant had been taken so completely by surprise that before the day's end, the Union army nearly wound up in the river! Some of Buell's troops had arrived the night before, but Grant himself wasn't even at Pittsburg Landing. When he heard the heavy gunfire, he had to take a quick boat trip from his headquarters at Savannah, Tennessee.

The fighting was brutal and costly. Many of the men on both sides had never been in battle before. Some of them ran in fright. Yelled an Illinois veteran as encouragement, "Why, it's just like shooting squirrels!" Said a Rebel soldier, "Oh God forever keep me out of such another fight."

Poor nervous Colonel Appler from Ohio. It did him little good to realize he had been correct when he reported enemy fire the day before. Now he stared into hundreds of gun barrels as the gray-clad Confederates moved directly toward him across the field. "This is no place for us," he declared and led his men in retreat to a ridge beyond the camp.

A few moments later, Sherman rode up with his orderly, a young private, Thomas D. Holliday of Illinois. Even the general had to admit that the enemy attack was real, especially when Holliday was killed and buckshot ripped through Sherman's hand. "Hold your position!" he shouted to a wide-eyed Appler and rode off.

Appler tried. But soon his group was attacked by the 6th Mississippi. The fighting was so savage that within a short time, 70 percent of the Mississippi troops were destroyed. Even so, they forced Appler into retreat.

An artist's depiction of the fighting at the well-named Hornets' Nest during the Battle of Shiloh.

Perhaps the whole Union army might have retreated under the fierce surprise attack. The fighting was so terrible along one Federal line of defense that bodies begin to pile up, some headless, some with limbs blown off by cannon fire. As a Confederate soldier fled the scene, he cried, "It's a hornets' nest in there." The name stuck and is given to that area of battle at Shiloh. For six long hours, 5,000 Northern troops held their positions against a withering series of attacks.

There was great courage and tenacity on both sides that Sunday, but it was the valor of the troops led by Sherman and others that bought Grant the time to bring up reinforcements. Each time the Rebels were driven back, a few precious minutes were saved for the North.

By mid-afternoon, Grant's army was badly battered and weakening, but still it held. Yet, General Johnston believed he was close to victory. At one point, he ordered a charge into a 10-acre peach orchard that was in full bloom. The men seemed reluctant to enter. Johnston, astride his horse, Fire-eater, slowly rode down the disheartened Rebel line, giving encouragement. Then he shouted, "I will lead you!" and galloped off toward the enemy, his men following. Soon the orchard rang with the sound of rifle fire and the sight of falling peach blossoms.

A short time later, Johnston was wounded in the leg and taken from his horse. The wound did not appear to be serious, although the general's boot was full of blood. In fact, the bullet had cut an artery in his right leg. A simple tourniquet—a bandage tightened to stop the flow of blood—would probably have saved him. But earlier, Johnston had sent his personal doctor, D.W. Yandell, to tend to his wounded men. Johnston even carried a tourniquet in his own pocket, but no one knew how to use it. A short time later, he bled to death.

At the end of the first day at Shiloh, Federal artillerymen stand by their 24-pound siege guns at Pittsburg Landing.

Beauregard assumed command. First, he ordered the general's death to be kept secret as long as possible for fear of demoralizing the troops. Then, he decided to smash into the center of the Northern line defending the Hornets' Nest.

Within moments, blue-clad men and their horses were hurled to the ground as a great onslaught of artillery began. Although it lasted but half an hour, the three or four rounds a minute seemed an eternity. It was obvious that the defenders could not hold out for long. Unit after unit was forced to break and pull back. Finally, the Hornets' Nest defense collapsed and the Confederates cheered themselves with victory.

Not quite. All during this stormy night as the battle raged, Grant was pulling the rest of his army into a new defense line back on Pittsburg Landing. At one point, after three horses were shot from under him, Sherman joined Grant, who was trying to catch a few minutes rest under a tree. Grant refused to sleep in his headquarters because he was so disturbed by the cries of the wounded lying there.

"We've had the devil's own day, haven't we?" said Sherman.

Dawn broke again on bloody Shiloh. It was Monday, April 7. An anxious Grant was cheered by the arrival of 6,000 fresh troops under command of Major General Lew Wallace, who had fought at Fort Donelson. The reinforcements gave new strength to the exhausted and weary Union men.

GRANT AT SHILOH

Disturbed by the criticism of his performance, General U.S. Grant later wrote this about the Battle of Shiloh: "The Battle of Shiloh, or Pittsburg Landing, fought on Sunday and Monday, the 6th and 7th day of April, 1862, has been perhaps less understood, or, to state the case more accurately, more persistently misunderstood, than any other engagement between National and Confederate troops during the entire rebellion....

"Shiloh was the severest battle fought at the West during the war, and but few in the East equaled it for hard, determined fighting. I saw an open field, in our possession on the second day, over which the Confederates had made repeated charges the day before, so covered with dead that it would have been possible to walk across the clearing, in any direction, stepping on dead bodies, without a foot touching the ground. On our side National and Confederate were mingled together in about equal proportions; but on the remainder of the field nearly all were Confederates. On one part, which had evidently not been plowed for several years, probably because the land was poor, bushes had grown up, some to the height of eight or ten feet. There was not one of these left standing unpierced by bullets. The smaller ones were all cut down."

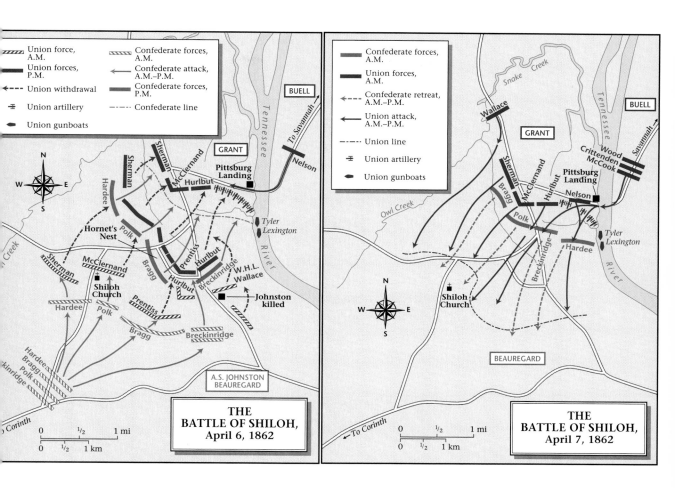

Legend (left map):
- Union force, A.M.
- Union forces, P.M.
- Union withdrawal
- Union artillery
- Union gunboats
- Confederate forces, A.M.
- Confederate attack, A.M.–P.M.
- Confederate forces, P.M.
- Confederate line

THE BATTLE OF SHILOH, April 6, 1862

Legend (right map):
- Confederate forces, A.M.
- Union forces, A.M.
- Confederate retreat, A.M.–P.M.
- Union attack, A.M.–P.M.
- Union line
- Union artillery
- Union gunboats

THE BATTLE OF SHILOH, April 7, 1862

The Confederates were equally exhausted and weary. Afraid that the fresh troops would reclaim victory, Beauregard headed for Pittsburg Landing and one last fight. But he had no fresh soldiers on his side. Tired beyond belief, the Rebels were cut down by the continuous barrage of fire from the Union troops.

Beauregard issued an order to withdraw, saying "the victory is sufficiently complete." Although it was later said that the South could have gained total victory, that appears doubtful against the thousands of reinforcements that joined the North at Shiloh.

Darkness fell, and the night echoed with the sounds of wounded men. "This night of horrors," said a Confederate

The brutal two-day Battle of Shiloh, while won finally by Grant's army, cost the lives of 3,500 soldiers.

soldier, "will haunt me to my grave." Medicine was scarce and infection spread rapidly. The sick list eventually reached 18,000. By the morning light of the third day, Grant walked about a battlefield littered with the bodies of both Union and Confederate soldiers.

More than 100,000 men fought at Shiloh, the little place of peace in the flowering peach orchard. Dead, wounded, and missing totaled more than 13,000 for the North and nearly 11,000 for the South. This was the most costly of Civil War battles to date.

Both sides were shocked at the casualty totals. Although the South had pushed back the North at the Hornets' Nest, the Rebels could not claim total victory. Indeed, the casualty figures totaled some 27 percent of the Confederate army at Shiloh. As

General Grant is shown here leading a desperate charge against the Confederate forces during the Battle of Shiloh.

George Washington Cable, soldier and novelist, said later, "The South never smiled again after Shiloh."

The North was victorious at Pittsburg Landing on April 7, regaining what it had held before. But what a terrible price. Although the battle at Shiloh did stop the Confederate attempt to conquer western Tennessee, Grant was called a butcher for allowing his army to be taken by surprise. More than that, he lost his command. As explanation, his superior, General Henry Halleck, quietly spread the rumor that Grant, a heavy drinker, had been drunk at Shiloh. Perhaps Halleck was smarting over the praise Grant had received at Fort Donelson. Perhaps it was just that Grant had proved to be an incompetent leader in the battle of the peach orchards, and so many had died.

Halleck, who had been given command of Federal forces in the west a month earlier, cautiously proceeded south to Corinth. But the battered Confederate army was in no condition to fight. Northern troops occupied an empty town when they took Corinth on May 30.

Grant was disgraced, so he decided to resign his commission and go home. Sherman, however, talked him out of it. This would prove to be significant for the North.

On to Richmond:

The Peninsula Campaign
April–July 1862

George B. McClellan, General-in-Chief of the Federal Armies, was not a happy man. It's never a good idea to displease your boss, but when your boss happens to be the President of the United States, there is extra cause for concern. And McClellan's boss, President Lincoln, was indeed displeased. In fact, he had been unhappy with McClellan for some time. When was the General going to move his troops somewhere? When was the U.S. army going on the offensive?

For his part, McClellan didn't like Lincoln either and was incredibly rude to him and other civilian leaders. He once wrote that the President was a "well-meaning baboon." Actually, McClellan, a dedicated Democrat, detested all Republicans, the administration, and anyone who was in favor of freedom for the slaves.

Not surprisingly, McClellan was not in good favor with several Republican leaders, including the new Secretary of War Edwin M. Stanton. They regarded him as slow, perhaps even reluctant, to fight. Some even hinted that he might be pro-Confederate.

Earlier in the year, the President had taken a most unusual step. He issued General War Order No. 1. In so many words it told all U.S. naval and land forces to get moving! A second order was even more direct. It told McClellan to attack the army of General Joseph E. Johnston at Manassas Junction, Virginia, and then march south to capture the Confederate capital of Richmond.

McClellan didn't much like the plan. Why attack Joe Johnston if he could avoid him and still get to Richmond? So, McClellan offered his own plan. He would float his huge army down Chesapeake Bay to the town of Urbanna at the mouth of the Rappahannock River. From there, he would march overland west to Richmond.

Lincoln didn't much like that plan. With McClellan's troops gone, who was going to protect the city of Washington from Johnston's army? When McClellan assured the President that he would leave behind ample troops, Lincoln agreed.

It was all downhill from there. Part of the plan involved sending troop-carrying boats through the lock on the Chesapeake and Ohio Canal. The men reached the lock only to find that the boats were six inches too wide to pass through.

The usually mild-mannered Lincoln was furious. Said he with uncharacteristic anger, "Couldn't the General have known whether a boat would go through that lock

GENERAL GEORGE B. McCLELLAN

George Brinton McClellan (1826–1885), was born in Philadelphia and graduated first in his class at West Point in 1846. He resigned his army commission in 1857 to become a railroad executive but was commissioned a major general at the start of the Civil War. After the Union's defeat at First Bull Run, he took command of the Department of the Potomac and became General-in-Chief of the Federal Armies in November 1861. A brilliant organizer who held total respect from his troops, he proved too cautious a commander, often refusing to take the offensive. For this, he would be relieved of command after Antietam in 1862.

General George Brinton McClellan.

before spending a million dollars getting them there? ... it seems to me that if I wished to know whether a boat would go through a hole ... common sense would teach me to go and measure it."

McClellan's troubles weren't over. General Joe Johnston, of course, had heard that the Union planned to attack him. So, he simply moved his troops out of Manassas Junction to a stronger position behind the Rappahannock River. McClellan had intended to land his men in that area. The result was a dead plan and much embarrassment.

Everyone, it seemed, was now disgusted with McClellan. Wrote Senator William P. Fessenden of Maine in a letter to his family, "... General McClellan is utterly unfit for his position....And yet the President will keep him in command and leave our destiny in his hands....Well, it cannot be helped. We went for a rail-splitter, and we have got one." The "rail-splitter" was a slap at Lincoln's humble beginnings.

As it turned out, the "rail-splitter" wasn't quite so willing to leave the country's destiny completely in McClellan's hands. McClellan was removed as General-in-Chief of the Federal Armies on March 11, 1862. He did, however, retain command of the huge Army of the Potomac. For the time being, there would be no Union general-in-chief, and all generals would report directly to Stanton.

WHERE'S MY ARMY?

McClellan wasn't the only one in trouble when Confederate troops pulled out of Manassas Junction. General Joe Johnston had not gotten around to informing his boss, Confederate president Jefferson Davis, that he was leaving. As a result, Lincoln knew Johnston had moved before Davis did. In fact, Davis sent a telegram promising reinforcements at Manassas the day after Johnston's army had evacuated.

Furious at his demotion, McClellan nevertheless vowed to fight the good fight. He offered a new plan. The objective of this so-called Peninsula Campaign was still the Confederate capital of Richmond, Virginia. But the approach was different.

McClellan decided it would be foolish to march his army due south overland to Richmond. To do so would be to run into the full strength of the Confederates. Instead, he now proposed to sail past Urbanna down the Rappahannock River, out into Chesapeake Bay, and land at the tip of the Virginia peninsula, formed by the York and James Rivers. Naturally, such a landing could take place only with the full protection of the navy. The army would embark at old Fort Monroe. Amazingly, it was in Yankee hands, even though the South held the city of Norfolk, just three miles across the water. From there, Federal troops would march straight up the peninsula to Richmond—about 70 miles to the northwest. And they would avoid Johnston and his army.

Lincoln was reluctant. Once again, he was worried about leaving the Federal capital unprotected. Once again, he was told that adequate forces would be left behind for safety. Thus assured, the impatient, frustrated President agreed.

McClellan was overjoyed! He felt he was back in Lincoln's good graces. He spoke of the President as "my strongest friend." In his excitement, however, McClellan seems to have forgotten his promise to protect Washington, D.C. As the Army of the Potomac moved out, Secretary Stanton couldn't find anyone on guard duty! So, he called back some troops to protect the capital. Among them was the corps led by none other than General McDowell, who had been removed after Bull Run.

Depleted somewhat in size, the still immense Army of the Potomac set out for Fort Monroe. Although numbers differ, anywhere from 100,000 to 120,000 men were involved in this Peninsula Campaign. A great flotilla of 400 vessels carried the troops back and forth, along with about 1,150 wagons, 15,000 horses and mules, 74 ambulances, 44 batteries of artillery, and incredible amounts of wire, tents, pontoon bridges, and anything else an army needs.

McClellan breathed confidence. Riding on his horse, Dan Webster, he supervised the most minute details of the expedition. "Rely on it that I will carry this thing through handsomely," he wrote to Secretary Stanton.

By the first week in April 1862, as the Confederates were about to surprise Grant at Shiloh, the Army of the Potomac was pouring ashore at Fort Monroe. But confident General McClellan was headed for trouble once more.

At the beginning of the campaign, McClellan, who was much loved by his troops, told them, "I am to watch over you as a parent over his children...." He also said, "I will bring you now face to face with the rebels...." That is, of course, if he could get them out of the mud. The General had been assured that all Virginia roads in the area were passable at any time. But the troops stepped off the boats into red clay that, with the aid of a few rain showers, quickly turned into sticky goo. Complained a young soldier, "It was like walking with 10 pounds of weight on each foot." One officer later said that a mule was swallowed in the goo right up to its ears, but that may have been an exaggeration!

In addition, McClellan's maps were terrible. Streams that weren't supposed to be there suddenly cropped up and had to be crossed. Roads turned out to be swamps, and some just weren't there at all.

Still confident, McClellan pressed on. To reach Richmond, he planned to march his army from Fort Monroe up the peninsula and establish a base at West Point, at the head of the York River. Somewhere between West Point and Richmond, he expected the decisive battle for the city to be fought.

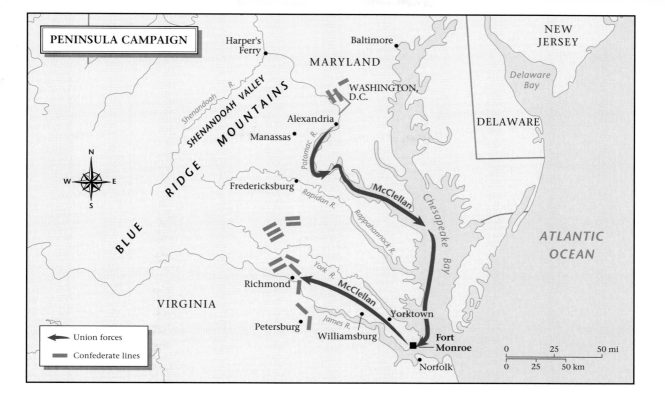

There was one minor obstacle on the way to West Point, however. Yorktown, at the mouth of the York River, was held by the Confederates. But surely, McClellan reasoned, its capture would be a rather easy task. Yorktown and Gloucester Point, just across the York, were defended by 11,000 to 15,000 Rebels, no match for the mighty Army of the Potomac. Or so it seemed.

The Confederate troops at Yorktown may have been small in number, but they had a big plus in leadership. He was Major General John Bankhead Magruder, a rather showy chap who enjoyed his nickname of Prince John. A successful actor before the war, he now used his theatrical talents to the limit.

McClellan's advance guard reached Yorktown on April 5. The Confederates had built high earthworks as protection. Ironically, it was at Yorktown 80 years earlier that the British had surrendered to General George Washington and ended the American Revolution. Now, the South was trying to bring about a successful revolution of its own.

General McClellan began his campaign aimed at the taking of Richmond by moving his troops down the Potomac River and Chesapeake Bay and then overland between the York and James Rivers toward the Confederate capital.

49

As the Yankees approached, Magruder marched one battalion of men in and out of protected areas, coming in full view of the Federal troops. Around and around, in and out went the same battalion, until the Yanks became convinced that Yorktown was defended by massive forces. In addition, Prince John kept his widely scattered artillery firing and the Confederate band playing even after dark. Wrote one lad from Alabama some days later, "[We] have been traveling most of the day, seeming with no other view than to show ourselves to the enemy at as many different points of the line as possible. I am pretty tired."

It was perhaps pure show business, but against the cautious McClellan, it worked. He telegraphed Washington that he was facing "probably not less than 100,000 men." Then he called for reinforcements and settled back to prepare for a long siege.

At any time, McClellan could most surely have taken Yorktown. Instead, he made plans—for one month. He also ignored President Lincoln's telegram that stated, "I think you had better break the enemy's line ... at once."

On May 4, 1862, McClellan was finally prepared to fire his artillery. On that day, General Joe Johnston, who had moved his army down the peninsula, evacuated Yorktown. That, too, was a surprise to McClellan. Nonetheless, he was jubilant. "Our success is brilliant," wired the general, "and you may be assured that its effects will be of the greatest importance. There will be no delay in following up the rebels."

Federal military supplies piled up at Ship Point near Yorktown, Virginia, waiting for General McClellan and a battle that never actually happened.

The following day, May 5, the Army of the Potomac actually got to fight someone. As Johnston continued to retreat toward Richmond, McClellan's forward units clashed with Confederate troops under Major General James Longstreet at Williamsburg. After a long day of heavy fighting with many casualties, the Rebels left. Northern troops occupied what had once been the colonial capital of Virginia. Now, the armies on both sides headed for Richmond, about 50 miles away.

In 1861, Lincoln appointed aeronaut and inventor Thaddeus Lowe as chief of the corps of aeronautics of the U.S. Army. Here one of Lowe's observation balloons, the Intrepid, *is being inflated.*

As the armies marched, there was action elsewhere. Union troops under command of Benjamin Butler—with a big boost from the U.S. Navy—took the city of New Orleans, Louisiana. His rough treatment of the city's citizens and Confederate claims that his government was corrupt would later bring cries of protest. In the wake of McClellan's army, Confederates abandoned the city of Norfolk and destroyed the ironclad *Merrimac*, so it would not fall into enemy hands. Federal troops took Pensacola, Florida, and Baton Rouge, Louisiana. With the enormous Army of the Potomac on the way, hundreds of citizens left the city of Richmond, including President Davis's wife and four children. And what of General McClellan? He waited. Apparently not yet convinced that he held the superior force, he requested McDowell's 40,000 troops in order to attack Richmond. Secretary of War Stanton was nearly speechless with anger! However, he found his voice enough to say, "If he had a million men, he would swear the enemy had two millions, and then he would sit down in the mud and yell for three!" McClellan's own men began referring to him as the "Virginia creeper."

In any case, McClellan wasn't getting 40,000 more troops. McDowell wasn't coming. The reason was Stonewall Jackson, who rightly could be considered a Confederate hero in the Peninsula Campaign even though he was out in the Shenandoah Valley, west of the Blue Ridge Mountains. Jackson's purpose was to confuse the Federals and keep them from reinforcing McClellan's army. This he did in superb fashion. He marched some 400 miles up and down the valley, a swift attack here, an ambush there. With just 17,000 men, he inflicted 7,000 casualties, captured much needed supplies, kept the Union armies confused and busy, convinced Federal leaders that he might well attack Washington, and made sure that McDowell and his 40,000 troops stayed away from Richmond.

This was a masterful performance by a leader whose own men often regarded as crazy. He preferred standing up most of the time because he thought that sitting put his internal organs "out of alignment." He sucked lemons even in battle. He said that pepper made his left leg ache, and he often walked around with one hand in the air to keep his balance. Jackson's men did not love him, but they certainly were willing to fight for—and with—him. To say the least, he was one of the South's—and the war's—most colorful participants.

By the end of May, the Army of the Potomac had actually moved to about 10 miles east of Richmond. McClellan's troops were divided by the rain-swollen Chickahominy River. On Saturday, May 31, General Johnston attacked the smaller of the Federal forces. The two-day battle at Fair Oaks, called Seven Pines in the South, ended in a draw, leaving both sides just about where they were before. Except for the casualties, of course. The

North lost some 5,000 men, the South about 6,000. The scene was so horrendous that McClellan himself wrote, "I am tired of the sickening sight of the battlefield."

The battle at Fair Oaks, or Seven Pines, may have been a standoff, but it had enormous consequences for both sides. For during the fight, General Joseph E. Johnston was badly wounded. President Davis had to find a new leader for the defense of Richmond. In this way and for the first time, one of the most famous of all Civil War names took charge of a major army. He was General Robert E. Lee. He would command the most noted of all Confederate forces, which he renamed the Army of Northern Virginia, until the end of the war.

An artist's view of the fighting on May 31, 1862, of the two-day Battle of Fair Oaks or Seven Pines.

Said Johnston of Lee's promotion, "The shot that struck me down was the best ever fired for the Confederacy." Said McClellan, "I prefer Lee to Johnston—[Lee] is too cautious ... when pressed by heavy responsibility ... is likely to be timid in action." McClellan might well have been speaking of himself.

Until now, Lee's service in the war had not been particularly outstanding. He had lost western Virginia in what was essentially a hopeless situation to begin with. He had been Davis's military adviser but with little real authority. Now he was in charge. Most of his fellow officers didn't expect much. He was regarded by some as "too fussy" and by others as just another big name from the prewar army who hadn't lived up to his press notices. In a short time, however, General Lee would earn the everlasting respect of most all who fought for him—and fought against him.

Lee took to his new post with zeal. When asked by Davis where the army should make a stand once Richmond had been taken, the general replied, "Richmond must not be given up. It shall not be given up."

Brave words for the leader of an army of about 60,000 men against an enemy perhaps twice that size. Lee's troops were, in general, poorly equipped and poorly disciplined. The Army of the Potomac was, in general, well equipped and well trained. It didn't take a military genius to see how the battle for Richmond would end.

But even a sure thing isn't always a sure thing. At this point, McClellan decided on caution again. Depressed by the bloody standoff at Fair Oaks and slowed by the constant rain, he hesitated. He needed time to rebuild bridges and bring up his big guns. He also kept calling for McDowell's troops as reinforcements. This gave Lee some precious time to tighten discipline among his own troops and get them better rations and uniforms.

On June 25, 1862, General McClellan attacked at Oak Grove, a small skirmish that put him about five miles from Richmond. It marked what came to be known as the Seven Days' Battles—at Mechanicsville, Gaines's Mill, Savage's Station, Frayser's Farm, and Malvern Hill, with smaller battles in-between— the new and last days of the Peninsula Campaign.

On June 26, as McClellan was getting ready to fight at Mechanicsville, Lee surprised him by attacking. Although the Rebels could not dislodge the Union soldiers from their high ground positions, that night the Yanks pulled back. On June 27, a five-hour fight at Gaines's Mill spelled victory for the South, sending the Federals back across the Chickahominy. Still the North consolidated its forces over the next two battles, and ended the Seven Days' Campaign at Malvern Hill with a victory.

The cost of the Seven Days battles was enormous on both sides. The North totaled some 16,000 casualties, the South about 20,000. Richmond remained in Confederate hands. Although he had won all but one battle during the Seven Days, McClellan continued to retreat. By July 3, he had reached Harrison's

In spite of Lee's brilliant efforts and McClellan's tendency to retreat, the Union won all but one of the battles between June 26 and July 2. However, the Union drive was halted just 25 miles from its goal of Richmond.

CAPTAIN SALLY

Sally Louisa Tompkins (1833-1916), a wealthy Virginia woman, became the only female army captain of the Confederacy. At the beginning of the war, she turned her large house in Richmond into a hospital for soldiers and ran it at her own expense. When enough military hospitals had been built in the South, President Davis ordered the private hospitals closed. However, he made Sally Tompkins a captain in the Confederate cavalry so that she could continue to run her hospital with the cooperation of the military.

In its four years, Captain Sally's hospital treated over a thousand soldiers, and amazingly only 75 died— by far the best record of the war. Sally Louisa Tompkins was buried with military honors in Richmond.

Men of the 3rd Vermont who survived the Seven Days' fighting visit the graves of their less fortunate comrades.

Landing on the James River. When urged to counterattack the Rebels, McClellan refused. He seemed to have become unnerved by Lee's surprise tactics. He told the President that he had not lost the battle for Richmond, but had "failed to win only because [he was] overpowered by superior numbers."

Lincoln told his commander to return to defend the city of Washington. On July 11, the President named Major General Henry W. Halleck the new General-in-Chief of all U.S. land forces. On August 14, McClellan obeyed Halleck's order to withdraw his Army of the Potomac from the Virginia peninsula.

Despite its many victories, McClellan's mighty army was battered and bruised. It was, for the present, effectively out of action. The much-heralded Peninsula Campaign had not achieved its objective, and the casualties on both sides seemed enormous. General McClellan's standing with his superiors could not have been lower. Now, for a brief and tragic time, the fortunes of General Robert E. Lee and the South would burn brightly.

But first, there was Second Bull Run.

Second Bull Run:

Same Ending
August 29–30, 1862

With the end of the Seven Days, a brief calm settled over the battlefields. General U.S. Grant had not resigned from the army. With good deportment, he was gaining favor once again with his superiors and was planning an offensive in Mississippi. McClellan was still at Harrison's Landing on the James River. And the newly designated commander of the Federal Army of Virginia, General John Pope, was getting ready to launch an offensive.

General Halleck had ordered McClellan to join Pope, camped on the north side of the upper Rappahannock River. Since Pope held the bridge crossings, his position was secure. General Lee knew that time was on the side of the Union. All Pope had to do was wait for McClellan. Lee could not hope to beat the combined armies. So, he had to get Pope before McClellan arrived. To this end, the daring Lee did just what the military textbooks say not to do in the presence of the enemy—divide your forces. But if ever there was a military man who knew how and when to break the rules, it was Robert E. Lee.

Lee sent half of his troops, with Stonewall Jackson at the head, to swing around the northwest behind the Bull Run Mountains. The other half, with Major General James Longstreet in immediate command, kept Pope occupied from across the Rappahannock.

GENERAL JOHN POPE

Brigadier General John Pope (1822–1892) was not much liked by his fellow officers. They thought him arrogant and a braggart. In an effort to demonstrate his mobility as a commander, he often boasted that his headquarters were in his saddle. To this, fellow officers responded that Pope had his headquarters where his hindquarters should have been. The South hated him for his treatment of civilians since he encouraged his troops to steal from Virginia farms. President Lincoln, however, gave command of the army in Virginia to this Kentucky-born West Point (1842) graduate. Impressed with Pope's string of small victories in the west, Lincoln thought that—at last—he had a commander who was willing to move. After Second Bull Run, however, Pope, as had other Northern leaders before him, lost his command.

General John Pope

A detachment of Pope's army, under Major General Nathaniel Prentiss Banks, had already met Jackson, on August 9, at Cedar Mountain, Virginia. After a sharp battle, the Federals were forced to retreat. Shortly after, another detachment had raided Pope's headquarters and got away with $35,000 in cash and the general's dress coat. That really annoyed the vain Pope! But the real insult came when Jackson's troops, after a two-day march, suddenly popped up about 20 miles behind Pope's forces. They not only raided Pope's supply depot at Manassas Junction, but they cut his supply lines to Washington!

This was too much. Now, Pope did just what Lee wanted him to do. He set out after Jackson. Generals Lee and Longstreet followed.

Angered, annoyed, and itching to fight, General Pope vowed to "bag the whole crowd" and destroy Jackson. Trouble is, he couldn't find him. Colorful Stonewall had just disappeared.

Actually, Jackson and his men, concealed by woods and hills, were camped near the site of the first battle, 10 months earlier, at Bull Run, or Manassas. On the night of August 28, 1862, Pope heard the sound of guns a few miles to the west in the area of Groveton, or Brawner's Farm. He was delighted! It meant that Jackson was found and, Pope believed, was in retreat from the division under Brigadier General Rufus King. Pope also believed that General Irvin McDowell and his men were fast approaching. He was wrong on three counts. Jackson was not in retreat, but had attacked King. McDowell had pulled another disappearing act. And Lee and Longstreet were fast approaching, not the phantom McDowell. In fact, Longstreet joined Jackson during the night.

General John Pope was a confused man and remained rather steadfastly so. On Friday morning, August 29, 1862, Pope attacked Jackson to begin the Battle of Second Bull Run, or Second Manassas.

The fighting was hard and furious. But the South had an advantage. Its only enemy was the North. In contrast, the North had to contend with not only the Confederates, but its own inept leadership. Pope, now aware that Longstreet had arrived but still in the dark about Lee, sent an order to two of his officers, Fitz-John Porter and Irvin McDowell. The elusive McDowell had finally emerged from the woods that morning. The order directed them to march west to Gainesville, which would take them right through Longstreet and his army. Porter was uneasy about this. He said to McDowell, "I don't think I can advance without provoking a battle." Replied McDowell, "I thought that was what we came here for."

For his part, McDowell had also received a message that morning from one of his cavalry commanders. It reported the advance of 17 regiments and 500 cavalry passing through

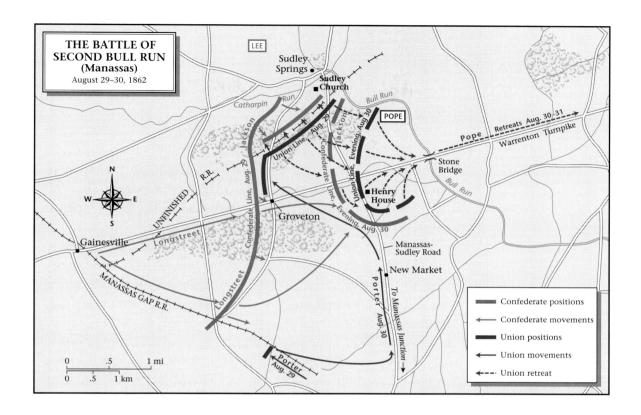

THE BATTLE OF SECOND BULL RUN (Manassas)
August 29–30, 1862

Gainesville. This could only have been the arrival of Lee's army. Incredibly, McDowell did not inform Pope of this report. In any event, Pope's order to Porter and McDowell was so loosely worded that neither man acted on it.

By the afternoon, Jackson and his men were under heavy attack. When they began to run out of ammunition and hurled rocks at the enemy, Pope was convinced of victory.

On the morning of August 30, Pope sent a message to Washington. It said that the Union army was victorious, that the enemy was in retreat, and he was about to pursue. Rarely has a general been more wrong.

Pope seemed to have a talent for ignoring what he did not wish to hear. When he was finally told of what was apparently

More self-confident than McClellan, John Pope was still out-maneuvered by Confederate Generals Longstreet and Jackson, and the second battle at Bull Run was lost by the Union army.

Lee's army passing through Gainesville, he dismissed the report. When he was told by Porter that there was a large enemy force in front of him—what turned out to be Longstreet and his 30,000 men—he ignored that, too.

But not for long. At about 4 p.m. that afternoon, according to reports, General Pope finally "showed some surprise." What was surprising him was the sight of gray-clad troops advancing on his left flank. Longstreet and his men attacked.

The rout was on. The Battle of Second Bull Run, like the First, was lost by the North. By nightfall, the Federal army was beaten and in retreat. Some 25,000 men were killed, wounded, or missing after Second Bull Run, nearly five times the number that had so horrified the country the year before.

General Pope was in disgrace, although he tried hard to blame the Union failure at Bull Run on Fitz-John Porter for not obeying his confusing order. In fact, Porter was court martialed

Federal troops scribbled their names and their regiments on the walls of this small house of worship in Falls Church, Virginia.

and dismissed from the army. His name was cleared, however, some 20 years later. As for Pope, he was sent on to a new command in Minnesota, but his significant role in the Civil War was over.

Amazingly enough, the Federal officer who benefited from the defeat at Bull Run was none other than George McClellan. He had sent his men on to Bull Run, but himself had been in Alexandria during the battle. With a great deal of reluctance, Lincoln put him back in command of the Army of the Potomac. Who else was there? At least his men loved him. "We must use the tools we have," said the President when the members of his Cabinet objected. Secretary of War Stanton and others believed that McClellan actually had been slow in forwarding his troops to the battle in the hope that Pope would be defeated. McClellan, of course, was jubilant. And not particularly modest. Wrote the general to his wife, "Again, I have been called upon to save the country."

ANGEL OF THE BATTLEFIELD

Clara Barton: Angel of the Battlefield (1821–1912). This founder of the American Red Cross (president 1882–1904) was a Massachusetts-born schoolteacher and later patent office clerk in Washington, D.C. Barely five feet tall, she began her health care work during the Civil War, saying, "While our soldiers stand and fight, I can stand and feed and nurse them." She administered to the wounded and dying at Cedar Mountain, Second Bull Run, and Antietam, among others. Of Second Bull Run, she said, "The men were brought down from the field... till they covered acres. By midnight there must have been three thousand helpless men lying in that hay...." At Antietam, while artillery fire burst all about the field hospital and male assistants ran for cover, she stood her ground at the surgeon's table holding it steady. Wrote the surgeon later to his wife, "In my feeble estimation, General McClellan, with all his laurels, sinks into insignificance beside the true heroine of the age, the angel of the battlefield."

Clara Barton (above)

FAITH IN GENERAL LEE

One reason why the badly outnumbered, generally more poorly equipped Confederate army was often so successful in battle was the trust and regard the average Southern soldier had for his commander. Nowhere was this more true than for those who served under Robert E. Lee. Here is part of a letter from John Hampden Chamberlayne, graduate of the University of Virginia, written to his mother on Saturday, September 6, 1862, just a few days after Second Bull Run.

"[The enemy] threw against our corps, all day long, vast masses of troops—Sigel's, Banks's, and Pope's own division. We got out of ammunition; we collected more from cartridge-boxes of fallen friend and foe; that gave out, and we charged with never-failing yell and steel. All day long they threw their masses on us; all day they fell back shattered and shrieking....I am proud to have borne my humble part in these great operations—to have helped, even so little, to consummate the grand plan, whose history will be text-book to all young soldiers, and whose magnificent success places Lee at the side of the greatest captains, Hannibal, Caesar, Eugene, Napoleon. I hope you have preserved my letters in which I have spoken of my faith in Lee. He and his round-table of generals are worthy of the immortality of Napoleon and his Marshals. He moves his agencies like a god—secret, complicated, vast resistless, complete."

General Robert E. Lee astride his beloved horse, Traveller.

Stonewall Jackson became an even greater hero to the South after Second Bull Run. Indeed, his performance throughout this entire campaign was perhaps the high point of his illustrious career. However, an even more illustrious victor was General Robert E. Lee. He had emerged from obscurity, taken a disorganized army, reshaped it, and led it to victory. A few months before, the enemy had been about to take the Confederate capital. Now, Lee and his men were very near that enemy's own capital city. It had been a remarkable summer for this great leader.

Brief and ultimately tragic though it might be, this was indeed a time of triumph for Lee and the Confederacy. Never before, and not again, would their dream of separation come so close. After a second, decisive victory at Bull Run, Lee was ready to move north. His next stop was a creek called Antietam.

Antietam:

The Bloodiest Day
September 17, 1862

With the war far into its second year, things were going unbelievably well for the Confederacy. Time and again, despite overwhelming numbers, the North was unable to press its advantage. Union generals seemed more intent on protecting territory than drawing the outnumbered enemy into the open. Instead, the South routed the North at Second Bull Run, and Southern troops invaded Kentucky and took Lexington. The North seemed to have lost control and was now fighting a defensive war. Worse still, Southern victories had caught the attention of Great Britain. Would the British grant recognition to the Confederates? If that happened, surely Southern independence would be secure. But British leaders were not known for haste. They would hold off on recognition a while longer, perhaps to see if General Lee could successfully invade the North.

To be sure, that's what Lee had in mind. In September, he crossed over the Potomac River into Maryland with his ragtag army. Rarely has there been a more unmilitary looking group— some shoeless, hardly any two dressed alike, dirty and vermin-infested, unshaved, in tatters, and hungry. They certainly did not look like conquering heroes. Nor were their leaders much better off. Stonewall Jackson was partly crippled from a bad fall that had injured his back. Generals John Hood and A.P. Hill were under arrest for quarreling with superior officers; Lee put them back on duty just before the battle. As for General Lee himself, he was in a bit of an embarrassing situation for a cavalryman. A few days earlier, he had tripped over the bridle of his horse, Traveller. Now both his hands were in splints and bandages, and he couldn't get up on Traveller without help.

Nonetheless, Confederate spirits were sky-high. They could sense victory. Hoping to get the neutral Marylanders to join them, Lee had his men sing "Maryland, My Maryland" as they marched. It didn't work, however, and most of the citizens stayed behind closed doors as the invaders passed by.

General George McClellan figured Lee to be heading for Baltimore or Washington. Actually, Lee was taking his men to Harrisburg, Pennsylvania, to capture the Union rail center there. General McClellan didn't know that, of course. But now McClellan got a break.

On Saturday morning, September 13, near Frederick, Maryland, a Union corporal happened to pick up a piece of paper in a meadow. It was wrapped around three cigars. The paper turned out to be a copy of Lee's plan for the Maryland campaign—the "lost order of Antietam." How it got there or got lost, no one knows.

McClellan learned that Lee was dividing his forces, sending half to Harpers Ferry under Jackson's command. With Lee's army fragmented, McClellan could move quickly, destroy the Army of Northern Virginia, and perhaps end the war right there.

But "quickly" was not a word in the cautious McClellan's vocabulary. It took him about 16 hours to get moving, even after discovering the paper. By this time, Lee had learned of the lost order and expected a battle at any moment. He took up positions along a quiet little creek called Antietam (pronounced an-tee-tam), just east of Sharpsburg. There he waited for the attack by McClellan and his overwhelmingly superior force.

Nothing happened. No artillery shots, no sound of rifles. Lee and his men waited in nervous anticipation. Then, all up and down the crest of the eastern bank along the Antietam, dark shadows began to appear. To the Confederates, the trees seemed to turn blue along the bank as the Union troops gathered and the blue line expanded as far as the eye could see.

Still, nothing happened. Many later said that had McClellan hurled his great army at Lee's men, the war might well have ended on this day. But the Union commander seemed content to check his battle plans and make sure everything was ready. Or perhaps he did not believe that Lee had so few men strung out along Antietam Creek. Whatever the reason, while the ever-cautious McClellan was checking battle plans, General Stonewall Jackson and his men were making a hard march from Harpers Ferry to join Lee. They did so on Tuesday, September 16.

But it was not until Wednesday, September 17, 1862, that McClellan launched his attack, and North met South in a savage battle. General Lee's 40,000 men opposed the more

General Lee's move north through western Maryland toward Harrisburg, Pennsylvania, was halted on September 15 at Sharpsburg, Maryland, by McClellan's forces.

LEE MARCHES NORTH

Hagerstown
Jackson
Antietam Sept. 17
Sharpsburg
Boonsboro
Turner's Gap
South Mountain Sept. 14
Frederick
McClellan Sept. 13
Crampton's Gap Sept. 14
Harpers Ferry Sept. 15
Lee Sept. 7
Lee Sept. 4-6
Shenandoah River
SHENANDOAH VALLEY
MARYLAND
Potomac River
VIRGINIA
Lee Sept. 2-3
Chantilly
Washington, D.C.
Centreville
McClellan

Union army
Union advance
Confederate army
Confederate advance

0   6   12 mi
0   6   12 km

than 75,000 Union troops under McClellan's command. This fight along Antietam Creek is called the bloodiest of the entire Civil War.

The Battle of Antietam was actually fought in three separate areas, which divided the superior Federal forces into smaller groups. The mist had hardly cleared that morning when Joseph "Fighting Joe" Hooker, a feisty major general from Massachusetts, charged into Miller's cornfield. He and his 8,600 infantrymen attacked Jackson and his 7,700 troops. The Yanks moved in a double line heading for a squat church on the hillside. It had been built by German Baptists called Dunkers. In front of the church, the Confederates had positioned a line of artillery.

Within minutes the cornfield was strewn with bodies, both Blue and Gray. The casualty list for the 12th Massachusetts alone was 224 men out of 334! Hooker was shot in the foot and had to be carried from the field. When Jackson sent in his reserves under General Hood, the Union assault was stopped. But the overall cost was terrible. Some 60 percent of Hood's men who fought in that cornfield also died in it. "Where is your division?" Hood was later asked. "Dead in the field," he replied.

Possession of Miller's cornfield changed hands many times that morning. By 10 a.m., 8,000 dead or

STONEWALL JACKSON'S WAY

As one of the Civil War's most colorful and well-known figures, Stonewall Jackson was not lacking in poetic tributes. This one was written after Antietam by John Williamson Palmer, a physician. Set to a rather lively tune, it said in part:

> Come, stack arms, men!
> Pile on the rails,
> Stir up the camp-fire bright;
> No matter if the canteen fails,
> We'll make a roaring night.
> Here Shenandoah brawls along,
> There burly Blue Ridge echoes strong,
> To swell the brigade's rousing song
> Of "Stonewall Jackson's Way."

The savage Battle of Antietam (or Battle of Sharpsburg) on September 17, 1862. The retreat of General Lee and his gallant Confederate forces gave Lincoln his opportunity to issue his preliminary Emancipation Proclamation.

wounded men from both sides lay sprawled among the cornstalks.

In the meantime, Lee had his forces entrenched along a sunken country road that once divided two farms. It quickly won the name of Bloody Lane. At first, the North had little success as unit after unit tried to break through. But finally, a breech was made at one point along the line, and the bodies of the Rebel troops began to pile up in the trench. The Confederates began to flee and it looked as though a Union victory was at hand. However, McClellan once more reacted cautiously and did not pursue the attack.

In the third battle of the day, General Ambrose Burnside, a personal friend of McClellan's, assaulted a strongly defended stone bridge over Antietam Creek. It would soon become known as Burnside's Bridge.

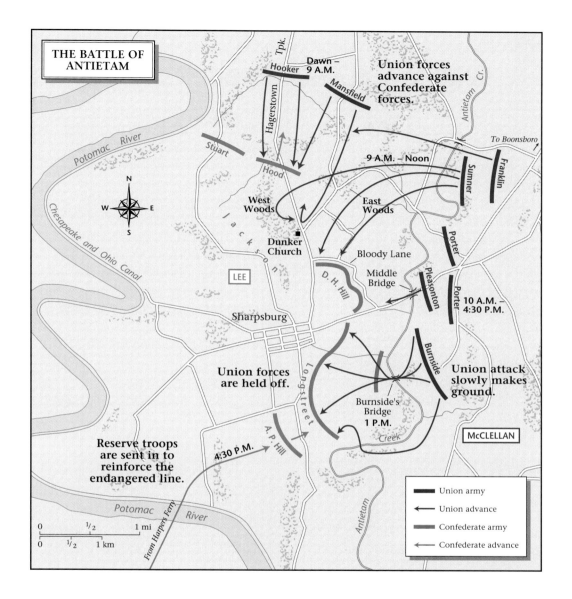

THE BATTLE OF
ANTIETAM

Union forces
advance against
Confederate
forces.

Dawn –
9 A.M.

Hooker

Mansfield

Hagerstown Tpk.

Stuart

Hood

9 A.M. – Noon

To Boonsboro

Sumner

Franklin

Potomac River

Chesapeake and Ohio Canal

West
Woods

East
Woods

Jackson

Dunker
Church

Bloody Lane

Middle
Bridge

LEE

D. H. Hill

Porter

Pleasonton

Porter

10 A.M. –
4:30 P.M.

Sharpsburg

Union forces
are held off.

Longstreet

Burnside

Union attack
slowly makes
ground.

Burnside's
Bridge
1 P.M.

Creek

McCLELLAN

Reserve troops
are sent in to
reinforce the
endangered line.

4:30 P.M.

A. P. Hill

Potomac River

From Harper's Ferry

Antietam

0   1/2   1 mi
0   1/2   1 km

	Union army
←	Union advance
	Confederate army
←	Confederate advance

At first this would seem an easy battle, Burnside's 12,500 men against 400 troops from Georgia under the command of Brigadier General Robert A. Toombs. But Toombs, who was Jefferson's secretary of state and had resigned to join the Confederate army, was a determined and unyielding man. He would not give in easily. Also, his troops held a favorable site above the stream.

Lee's invasion of Maryland was blocked at the savage Battle of Antietam. President Lincoln claimed a major victory. But McClellan failed to use his advantage to destroy the Confederate army and Lee's troops were able to retreat across the Potomac.

WHY SO MANY HAD TO DIE

One of the main reasons for the great number of deaths in so many Civil War battles was the state of medicine in the mid-nineteenth century. If a soldier didn't die from his wounds, he was likely to die of sickness. Doctors and nurses were woefully ignorant about germs. There were very few medicines and sanitation was practically unheard of. The troops drank contaminated water, which made them sick, and used uncovered ditches as bathroom facilities, which also made them sick. For every Union soldier killed in battle, four men died of sickness. And things were no better in the South. Five times as many Rebels got sick as got injured.

Author of *Little Women*, Louisa May Alcott volunteered to work in a Washington, D.C., hospital in 1862, until she contracted typhoid fever. This is what she remembered of the experience:

"There they were! 'Our brave boys,' as the papers justly call them, for cowards could hardly have been so riddled with shot and shell, so torn and shattered, nor have borne suffering for which we have no name.... Forty beds were prepared, many already tenanted by tired men who fell down anywhere and drowsed till the smell of food roused them.... One, with a gunshot wound through the cheek, asked for a looking glass, and when I brought one, regarded his swollen face... as he muttered—'I vow to gosh, that's too bad! I warn't a bad-looking chap before, and now I'm done for; won't there be a thunderin' scar? And what on earth will Josephine Skinner say?'"

Dead Confederate soldiers lie outside Dunkers' Church after the Battle of Antietam.

From their position over the bridge, the Confederates fought off the Union troops for some three hours. Wave after wave of blue rushed at the bridge, only to be driven back. Finally, however, aided by the fact that the Georgians were running out of ammunition, Burnside's men broke through and gained the bridge. Downstream, Federal troops crossed the Antietam and headed for Sharpsburg. A Union victory seemed certain.

From a nearby hilltop, General Lee watched through a telescope. When it seemed even to him that all was lost, he noticed a dusty column appearing from the south. He asked an aide what troops they were and was told, "They are flying Virginia and Confederate flags, sir."

And so they were. Some 3,000 footsore troops under command of the recently disgraced A.P. Hill had just marched from Harpers Ferry to join the fight. It was a strange but welcome sight to the South. Hill led his men in a bright red shirt, which he always wore in battle, and many of his troops were wearing the blue jackets of the Union. They had taken them from fallen soldiers to replace their own tattered clothes. Uncertain about what side was approaching, the North held fire and allowed Hill and his men to reinforce Lee.

Near Sharpsburg, a Union medical officer stands amid the makeshift tents erected for the wounded at Antietam.

The reinforced Confederates fought back against repeated attacks. They gave up ground grudgingly, but never quite retreated. Battered and weary, the Rebels were still fighting on the following day. McClellan once more did not renew the attack, and Lee led his ragtag troops back to Virginia. So ended the terrible Battle of Antietam.

Technically, this battle might almost be called a draw, but in fact the North had won a victory. The Southern advance northward was halted. The Union army had regained control. This was not unnoticed by the cautious British, who decided to hold off on recognizing Confederate independence. Recognition would never come. The South had lost a precious, opportune moment.

These Union nurses are dressed in their formal uniforms for the photographer. Heroic nurses on both sides tended to the constant streams of wounded men.

But how horrendous the cost. This was the single most deadly day of the war. Casualties for the North, including dead, wounded, and missing, totaled more than 12,000. Numbers for the South vary between 10,000 and more than 13,000. Even so, that would mean at least one-quarter of Lee's forces became casualties that day. Yet, his army had not been destroyed.

As the mist cleared the meadows on the morning of September 18, the bodies of the dead and wounded stretched as far as the eye could see. Here and there lay corpses of the officers' horses. The wounded were crowded into every available farmhouse or barn, or any structure that would provide shelter. It was a sight few of the living would ever forget.

Clara Barton said of Antietam: "I had to wring the blood from the bottom of my clothing before I could step, for the weight about my feet."

For a few days after Antietam, an impatient President Lincoln waited to see if McClellan would aggressively follow the retreating Southern troops. When he did not, Lincoln went to Sharpsburg himself on October 1. At McClellan's headquarters, Lincoln urged the general to get moving. McClellan seemed to agree.

By October 8, the war news looked a little better in Washington. Federal forces under Brigadier General Don Carlos Buell had stopped a second Confederate invasion of the North at Perryville, Kentucky.

On October 4, 1862, at Antietam, President Lincoln and General McClellan meet for a discussion in the general's tent.

But General McClellan was still sitting in Sharpsburg. He had, however, sent the President a few wires concerning "fatigued" horses as one reason why the army wasn't going anywhere. This so annoyed Lincoln that he sent a wire on October 25 to McClellan. It read: "Will you pardon me for asking what the horses of your army have done since the battle of Antietam that fatigues anything?"

The next day McClellan got his army in gear and slowly began to follow Lee across the Blue Ridge Mountains into Virginia. But Lincoln had had enough. On November 7, 1862, McClellan was relieved of command. The general seemed somewhat surprised and hurt at this action. Said he, "They have made a great mistake. Alas, for my poor country!"

AMBROSE BURNSIDE, SOLDIER AND FASHION ORIGINATOR

Ambrose Everett Burnside (1824–1881) sported magnificent side-whiskers, starting the fashion that became known by a reversal of his name—sideburns. Born in Liberty, Indiana, he graduated from West Point in 1847, resigning his commission in 1853 to make firearms in Rhode Island. He invented a breech-loading carbine and went back in the army during the Civil War, commissioned a brigadier general. After the war he became governor of Rhode Island (1866–1869) and a U.S. senator (1875–1881).

Ambrose Everett Burnside and his fine side-whiskers.

This was the end of George B. McClellan's military career. Little Mac, as he was affectionately known by his troops, reviewed them for the last time on November 10, 1862. Soldiers wept as he rode past. "Stand by General Burnside as you have stood by me," he told them, "and all will be well. Good-bye lads."

McClellan was told to return to his home in Trenton, New Jersey, and await further orders. They never came. In 1864, he ran for U.S. president on the Democratic ticket and lost to Lincoln. After serving as the governor of New Jersey (1878–1881), he spent his years writing and traveling until his death in Orange, New Jersey, in 1885.

It is not difficult to understand why the controversial McClellan was finally replaced. But why Ambrose E. Burnside as the new commander? True, he had finally taken the bloody bridge at Antietam, but at an awesome cost of lives. Burnside carried himself with an air of dignity befitting a leader. Yet, behind the impressive sideburns was an often indecisive, always anxious man who questioned his own competence under fire and had no desire whatsoever for a leadership role. In fact, he tried to turn it down, freely admitting that he had not the talent for such a position. At least one fellow officer must have agreed, for he wrote, "Few men have risen so high upon so slight a foundation."

Federal troops under General Burnside storm the bridge at Antietam Creek and attack Confederate positions on September 17, 1862.

Actually, when it came to choosing a new leader for the Army of the Potomac, President Lincoln really didn't have a lot of choices. He needed someone with experience, of course. There was Edwin V. Sumner. This major general had performed well at Antietam, but at age 65, some thought he was too old to take over the entire army. There was William B. Franklin, an able leader but afflicted with what Lincoln regarded as McClellan's problem—the "slows." There was the seemingly fearless Fighting Joe Hooker, but the President regarded him as too junior in command. That seemed to leave Ambrose Burnside. Sometimes the choice isn't always who's best, but who's best of what's there.

Competent or not, willing or not, Ambrose Burnside was now in the hot seat and under President Lincoln's watchful eye. Burnside had to do something. So, as the new commander of the Army of the Potomac, he reorganized his troops into divisions. The Right Grand division was placed under Major General Edwin V. Sumner, the Center Grand Division under Major General Joseph Hooker, and the Left Grand Division under Major General William B. Franklin.

Next, Burnside devised a plan. With the President's approval, he would march his army to the Confederate capital at Richmond, Virginia. Only two things stood in the way. One was General Robert E. Lee; the other was Fredericksburg.

Fredericksburg:

The Terrible Test
December 13, 1862

On September 22, 1862, shortly after the Battle of Antietam, President Abraham Lincoln issued the war's most important document, the preliminary Emancipation Proclamation. This proclamation called on the seceding states to return to the Union by the beginning of the new year. If they did not do so, all their slaves would be declared free. Although some historians doubt whether Lincoln actually had the power to issue such a declaration, it had important effects.

The Confederate states did not return to the Union. But the proclamation had other important consequences. It brought to the war a fight for human freedom. It also made any interference in the war by foreign powers virtually impossible. It was one thing for Britain to think about favoring the South to get cotton. It was quite another to interfere in a crusade for human freedom. Eventually it made thousands of former slaves available for recruitment into Union services. By war's end, 200,000 blacks, most of whom were freed slaves, had played a major role in Northern victories.

On January 1, 1863, the Emancipation Proclamation went into effect. It remains one of the nation's most important documents.

While both sides absorbed the news of the preliminary Emancipation Proclamation, General Ambrose Burnside left his headquarters near Warrenton in northern Virginia. In the cold

6

rain of late November 1862, he began to move his grumbling troops to the south along the Rappahannock River.

With Lincoln's approval, Burnside planned to march some 35 miles to the south, cross the Rappahannock River on pontoon bridges, take Fredericksburg, defeat Lee's army somewhere between there and Richmond, and win a clear path to the Confederate capital.

The general was filled with new determination. He would display the aggressive spirit so lacking in his predecessor. But aggressiveness did not come naturally to Ambrose Burnside. And when it did, it proved to be a disaster.

Everything went wrong, although not all could be blamed on Burnside. The key to his plan, of course, was to get to Fredericksburg and take the town before Lee could station his troops on the overlooking hills. But when Burnside and his 120,000 men arrived, he found the War Department had let him down. There were no pontoon bridges to get across the river. They took 17 days to arrive.

Under fire from Confederate forces, Union engineers build a pontoon bridge, in December 1863, across the Rappahannock River near Fredericksburg.

In the meantime, General Lee and his force of about 75,000 were not standing still. After Antietam, Lee had marched back across the Blue Ridge Mountains and south into Virginia. Now, three months later, Southern troops were spread out along a more than six-mile crest of hills looking down on Fredericksburg and the Rappahannock River. Lee commanded the middle of the line, with Stonewall Jackson to his right and General James Longstreet to the left. There, they waited.

While the North waited for bridges and the South waited for battle, the two sides sometimes shouted at each other in a rather goodnatured way. They even traded coffee, newspapers, sugar, or cigarettes, sent in little paper boats across the narrow river. At one point, the Federal band, after playing the "Star Spangled Banner" and other such tunes, struck up "Dixie." Both sides cheered and laughed. That was just about the end of the merriment, however.

Finally, in the morning fog on December 11, the Union army began constructing five pontoon bridges across the Rappahannock. They did so under deadly fire from the Rebel

LONGSTREET ON BURNSIDE

Sometime after the battle, General Longstreet wrote of his feelings about the Union commander at Fredericksburg: "I have been asked if Burnside could have been victorious at Fredericksburg. Such a thing was hardly possible. Perhaps no general could have accomplished more than Burnside did, and it was possible for him to have suffered greater loss. The battle of Fredericksburg was a great and unprofitable sacrifice of human life made, through the pressure from the rear, upon a general who should have known better and who doubtless acted against his judgment. If I had been in General Burnside's place, I would have asked the President to allow me to resign rather than execute his order to force the passage of the river and march the army against Lee in his stronghold."

THEY COULDN'T HAVE WON THE WAR WITHOUT HIM

No army, no matter how large or well trained, can win a battle without transportation. Getting men and equipment where they were supposed to be during the Civil War often became the responsibility of Herman Haupt (1817–1905), a West Point graduate (1835) and civil engineer. He was given the job of rebuilding and running the war-damaged railroads in northern Virginia. Once asked to construct a 400-foot-long bridge across the Potomac, he did so in just nine days, using inexperienced soldiers and some two million feet of green lumber. President Lincoln viewed the completed bridge and said, "It is the most remarkable structure that human eyes ever rested on. There is nothing in it but beanpoles and cornstalks."

In November 1862, Haupt told General Burnside that in order to get men and supplies to Fredericksburg by rail, the trains would have to run on a fixed schedule. That meant unloading the cars promptly and sending them back to be refilled. This was a new idea for the time and one not easily obeyed. To his great frustration, Haupt found that some officers simply removed the loaded freight cars and parked them in a warehouse. Worse still, the soldiers sometimes took the water that was intended for the boilers and washed their clothes instead. As a result, complained Haupt, "many engines are stopped on the road with foamy boilers." But his system finally won out and on the eve of Fredericksburg, some 800 tons of supplies were moving daily to Burnside's army.

Brigadier General Herman Haupt (above) and his 400-foot-long railroad bridge across the Potomac River.

troops. In turn, the Federals began to shell the town. The roar from their 200 cannons was deafening. Fortunately, Lee had urged the people of Fredericksburg to leave the area before the enemy arrived. Some 6,000 civilians had obeyed him.

It took until nightfall for a Northern division to occupy the town. By that time much of it was on fire. As they waited to meet the enemy, troops of the North engaged in an old, if one of the least heroic, of military customs. In true "to the victor belong the spoils" fashion, the town of Fredericksburg was looted and all but destroyed.

And the battle had not yet begun. In the darkness, General Lee waited on top of Marye's Heights. From there, he could look across the river at Chatham Mansion. Now taken over by Burnside for his headquarters, it was the place where, 30 years earlier, Lee had courted his wife, Mary Anne Randolph Custis.

It was still foggy by mid-morning on Saturday, December 13, 1862. The Battle of Fredericksburg began with an assault on Stonewall Jackson's Confederates from the Left Grand Division of General William Franklin. He was supposed to have attacked at dawn, but a mixup in orders had caused the delay. After a seesaw battle, a Union division briefly pierced Jackson's line, but was eventually driven back.

A bleak view of Marye's Heights where Rebels waited behind a stone wall to cut down Burnside's Union troops as they attacked.

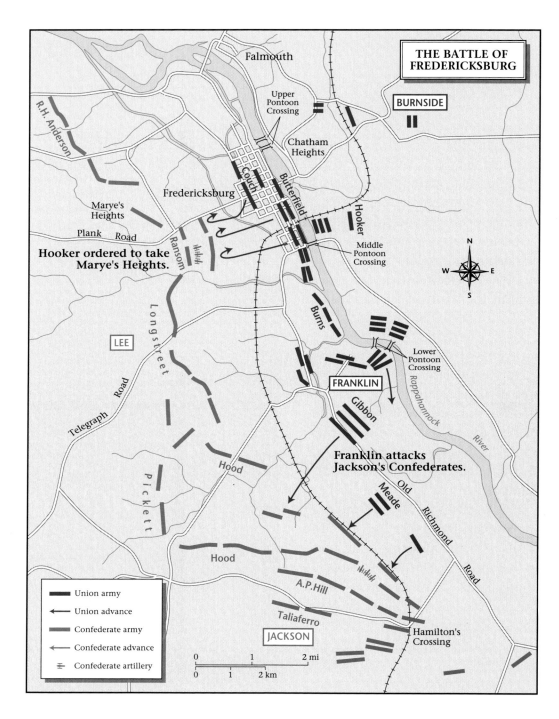

THE BATTLE OF FREDERICKSBURG

Falmouth

Upper Pontoon Crossing

BURNSIDE

R.H. Anderson

Chatham Heights

Couch

Butterfield

Fredericksburg

Marye's Heights

Hooker

Plank Road

Ransom

Hooker ordered to take Marye's Heights.

Middle Pontoon Crossing

LEE

Longstreet

Burns

Lower Pontoon Crossing

FRANKLIN

Rappahannock River

Telegraph Road

Gibbon

Hood

Franklin attacks Jackson's Confederates.

P I C K E T T

Meade

Old Richmond Road

Hood

A.P. Hill

Taliaferro

JACKSON

Hamilton's Crossing

	Union army
←	Union advance
	Confederate army
←	Confederate advance
	Confederate artillery

0   1   2 mi
0   1   2 km

After hours of bloody attack and counterattack and the death of thousands, Union troops had battled slightly beyond a destroyed Fredericksburg. However, when the fighting was over, the Confederates had forced the withdrawal of the Union army.

THE ERIN GO BRAGH! BRIGADE.

The Erin go bragh! Brigade. One of the many ironies of this "brother against brother" war involved the Second Brigade of the II Corps' 1st Division, Union army. Made up of men from Massachusetts, New York, and Pennsylvania, it was known as the Irish Brigade. Some 1,300 strong, they rushed the stone wall at Fredericksburg waving their emerald green flags with the gold shamrocks. Although they got within 25 paces under murderous fire, they were driven back. The Irish Brigade later counted 50 dead, 421 wounded, and 74 missing or captured. The enemy on the other side of the wall were men of the 24th Georgia. They were Irish, too.

In this Currier and Ives print Union troops are shown advancing on a Confederate position at Fredericksburg, December 13, 1862.

BURNSIDE BLUNDERS!

Here are two accounts, North and South, of the battle at Fredericksburg. Both blame General Burnside.

This account, by an unknown Union soldier, was published in a newspaper, the *Cincinnati Commercial*, on December 17, 1862. "It was not possible for anyone who had witnessed the fight, and was candid with himself, to dispute the fact that we had had the worst of it. We had started out to take the enemy's batteries on the hills. That we had done no such thing was painfully apparent... The city of Fredericksburg was a trap, and we had plunged into it. The policy of permitting us to 'occupy and possess' it under commanding batteries, was clear enough. The blunder stood revealed."

Here is part of a letter written by William Owen of the Washington Artillery of New Orleans: "After withdrawing from the hill the command was placed in bivouac, and the men threw themselves upon the ground to... rest. We had been under the hottest fire men ever experienced for four hours and a half, and our loss had been three killed and twenty-four wounded. Among them was Sergeant John Wood, our leading spirit in camp theatricals, who was severely injured.... One gun was slightly disabled, and we had exhausted all of our canister, shell, and case shot, and nearly every solid shot in our chests. At 5:30 another attack was made..., but it was easily repulsed, and the battle of Fredericksburg was over, and Burnside was baffled and defeated."

In the meantime, Burnside ordered General Joseph Hooker, with his Central Grand Division, to take Marye's Heights. When he saw the beginning onslaught of men in blue, Lee was astounded. Who would be so foolish as to attempt an attack at this site? The answer proved to be Burnside. The gray-clad Confederates were lined up behind a four-foot stone wall running all along the bottom of the hill. Behind the wall were four lines of infantrymen. Covering all of the Heights was amassed Confederate artillery. "A chicken could not live in that field when we open on it," said a Rebel soldier.

Some of Burnside's officers agreed. They urged the general to

rescind the order. It would be "murder, not warfare," they told him. But General Ambrose Burnside was determined to be aggressive this day.

A seemingly endless wave of Union soldiers marched toward Marye's Heights and the stone wall. As they neared the barricade, Rebel shots rang out, filling the air with smoke and screams of the wounded. Soon the meadow was black with the advancing men of the North, their bodies falling, as General Longstreet later remarked, "to the steady dripping of rain from the eaves of a house."

Brigade after brigade charged the stone wall. They seemed to "melt," said a Union officer, "like snow coming down on warm ground."

Few buildings remained untouched after the fierce Battle of Fredericksburg.

87

There was no doubt of the courage of the men on both sides. But the great assault planned by Burnside seemed more like a great slaughter. As fresh troops waited to storm the wall, they watched the bodies of the wounded dragged or carried from the meadow into the hastily constructed field hospitals.

It was a terrible, wild, and futile battle. As Lee watched from the Heights, he is said to have commented, "It is well that war is so terrible; we should grow too fond of it." That night, as the temperatures fell, men froze to death beside the bodies of those who had bled to death.

In the frigid December weather near Fredericksburg, Confederate sentries try to keep warm over a small fire.

The carnage was unbelievable. By day's end, losses for the Army of the Potomac—dead, wounded, and missing—totaled more than 12,000. Of the nearly 1,300 men killed, most had died in a badly planned attack that could not be won. Casualties for the South reached some 5,300.

Was it all worth it? What had been gained? Lee and his tired men stayed on the hills. Burnside and his shocked troops remained in the city.

The following day, weeping openly at the terrible cost, Burnside proposed to lead another attack on the Heights to avenge his failure. His officers talked him out of it.

A sullen, discouraged Army of the Potomac wearily withdrew across the Rappahannock. The Confederates did not try to advance their positions. From both sides of the river, the armies glared at each other, all thoughts of any merriment gone.

Technically, the North still held the meadow where so much of the fighting had taken place. So, they regarded the Battle of Fredericksburg as a victory. But it was a hollow one. Seldom have so many died for so little gain or meaning.

The Army of the Potomac and the North in general were plunged into depression and gloom. Everyone was blamed for the massacre at Fredericksburg, especially Burnside. Desertions for the North ran high. Said President Lincoln, "If there is a worse place than hell, I am in it."

As the year ended, the opposing armies were set for battle at Murfreesboro, or Stone's River, Tennessee, and General U.S. Grant was trying to devise a plan that would enable him to capture Vicksburg. The Army of the Potomac was about to get another new commander. President Lincoln was about to free the slaves. West Virginia was about to join the Union.

And as 1862 came to a close, the outcome of the war seemed to hang in the balance. Battered and sorely tested, the Confederate armies could take pride in their ability to withstand a numerically superior enemy. Depressed and disheartened by the massacre at Fredericksburg, Northern officers, led by a concerned President, settled back to take stock.

The fighting would go on. A final Federal victory was still a long, grief-filled time away. Many more had yet to die in this terrible and bloody adventure known as the American Civil War.

Chronology of Important Events

1860

November 6	Abraham Lincoln elected president.
November 9	South Carolina calls a secession convention.
November 15	Major Robert Anderson is sent to Charleston to take command of the Federal garrison at Fort Sumter.
December 20	South Carolina secedes from the Union.

1861

January 9	Mississippi secedes from the Union.
January 10	Florida secedes from the Union.
January 11	Alabama secedes from the Union.
January 19	Georgia secedes from the Union.
January 21	Jefferson Davis and four others resign from the U.S. Senate.
January 26	Louisiana secedes from the Union.
January 29	Kansas becomes 34th state.
February 1	Texas secedes from the Union.
February 9	Davis is elected provisional Confederate president.
February 18	Davis is inaugurated in Montgomery, AL.
March 4	Lincoln is inaugurated as the 16th President of the United States.
March 6	Davis calls for 100,000 volunteers.
April 12	Confederates fire on Fort Sumter; war begins.

April 13	Fort Sumter surrenders.
April 15	Lincoln calls for 75,000 volunteers.
April 19	Lincoln orders blockade of Confederate ports from South Carolina to Texas.
April 20	Robert E. Lee resigns from the U.S. Army. Confederates take abandoned Union navy yard at Norfolk, VA.
April 27	Lincoln includes ports of Virginia and North Carolina in blockade.
May 6	Arkansas secedes from the Union.
May 7	Tennessee secedes from the Union and joins the Confederacy.
May 13	Queen Victoria says Great Britain will stay neutral.
May 20	North Carolina secedes from the Union.
May 21	Confederates move capital to Richmond, VA.
May 23	Virginia secedes from the Union.
May 24	Federal troops occupy Alexandria, VA.
May 28	Brig. Gen. Irvin McDowell becomes Union commander, Dept. of Northeastern Virginia.
May 29	Federal troops occupy Newport News, VA.
June 10	Federal troops lose battle at Big Bethel, VA. Napoleon III says France will stay neutral.
July 11	Maj. Gen. George B. McClellan wins battle of Rich Mountain, VA.
July 21	South wins battle at First Bull Run (Manassas). Maj. Gen. John C. Fremont takes command of Union forces in the West.
July 27	McClellan replaces McDowell as Federal commander in Washington area.

August 10	Confederates win at Wilson's Creek, MO, defeating army of Brig. Gen. Nathaniel Lyon, who is killed in battle.
August 28	General U.S. Grant takes command of Federal troops in SE Missouri and southern Illinois.
August 29	Federal amphibious attack is successful at Hatteras Inlet, NC.
September 4	Columbus, KY, taken by Confederate Maj. Gen. Leonidas Polk.
September 6	Grant takes Paducah, KY.
September 10	Confederate Gen. Albert Sidney Johnston takes command of western armies.
September 17	Judah P. Benjamin becomes Confederate secretary of war; Thomas Bragg becomes Confederate Attorney General.
September 20	South captures garrison at Lexington, MO.
October 8	Brig. Gen. William T. Sherman takes command of Federal army in Kentucky.
October 21	South wins at Ball's Bluff, VA.
November 1	McClellan replaces Winfield Scott as Federal general in chief.
November 6	Davis elected to 6-year term as Confederate president.
November 7	Grant defeated at Belmont, MO.
November 8	North takes Port Royal, SC. U.S. imprisons Confederate commissioners Mason and Slidell in *Trent* Affair.
November 9	Brig. Gen. Don Carlos Buell replaces Sherman in Kentucky.
November 19	Maj. Gen. Henry W. Halleck takes command of Union troops in Missouri.
November 30	Britain demands release of Mason and Slidell.
December 27	Mason and Slidell released.

1862

January 11	Edwin M. Stanton becomes U.S. secretary of war.
January 19	Union controls eastern Kentucky with victory at Mill Springs.
February 6	Federal army-navy force attacks Fort Henry on the Tennessee River.
February 8	Union takes Roanoke Island, NC.
February 16	Fort Donelson, with 15,000 soldiers, surrenders to Grant.
February 22	Davis inaugurated as permanent president of the Confederacy.
February 25	South abandons Nashville, TN.
March 8	Union wins Battle of Pea Ridge, AR.
March 9	*Monitor* and *Merrimac* clash in indecisive battle of the ironclads, spelling the end of the "wooden" navy.
March 11	Halleck takes command of Federal forces in the West. McClellan removed as general in chief but retains Army of the Potomac.
March 12	Union navy occupies Jacksonville, FL.
March 14	Brig. Gen. Ambrose E. Burnside takes New Bern, NC.
March 17	Grant takes command of Federal army at Pittsburg Landing, TN. Davis reorganizes Cabinet with Judah P. Benjamin as secretary of state and George W. Randolph as secretary of war.
March 23	Maj. Gen. Thomas J. (Stonewall) Jackson defeated at Kernstown, VA.
April 5	McClellan attacks Confederates at Yorktown, VA.
April 6	Confederates defeat Grant's forces in surprise attack at Pittsburg Landing (Shiloh). Gen. A.J. Johnston is killed, replaced by Gen. P.G.T. Beauregard.

April 7   Confederates retreat from Shiloh, after defeat by U.S. forces.

April 8   Union Maj. Gen. John Pope takes Island No. 10 in Mississippi River.

April 16   Lincoln signs bill abolishing slavery in Washington, D.C.

April 25   David G. Farragut's Union naval forces capture New Orleans, LA.

May 1   Brig. Gen. Benjamin F. Butler occupies New Orleans and begins controversial administration.

May 4   Siege of Yorktown, VA, ends. Johnston retreats.

May 5   Maj. Gen. James Longstreet battles McClellan at Williamsburg, VA.

May 8   Jackson wins at McDowell, VA.

May 9   Confederates abandon Norfolk, VA, in face of Peninsula Campaign.

May 10   Union occupies Pensacola, FL.

May 11   *Merrimac* burned to prevent capture.

May 12   Union occupies Baton Rouge, LA.

May 25   Jackson is victorious at Winchester, VA.

May 30   Confederates retreat from Corinth, MS.

May 31   Inconclusive Battle of Fair Oaks (Seven Pines). Gen. Joseph Johnston is severely wounded.

June 1   General Robert E. Lee takes command of forces defending Richmond.

June 6   Federals take Memphis, TN.

June 8   Jackson is victorious at Battle of Cross Keys, VA.

June 9   Jackson takes Port Republic, VA.

June 19	Slavery abolished in U.S. territories.
June 25	McClellan starts Seven Days' Battles with attack at Oak Grove, VA.
June 26	Battle at Mechanicsville, VA. Pope takes command of Federal Army of Virginia.
June 27	Gen. Braxton Bragg commands Confederate Army of Mississippi in place of Beauregard. Battle at Gaines' Mill.
June 29	Battle at Savage's Station.
June 30	Battle of Frayser's Farm.
July 1	Malvern Hill battle ends Seven Days.
July 3	McClellan pulls back to Harrison's Landing, VA.
July 11	Halleck named general in chief of Union army.
July 22	Lincoln presents first draft of Emancipation Proclamation to Cabinet.
August 4	Lincoln calls for 300,000 militia.
August 9	Jackson victorious at Cedar Mountain, VA.
August 26	Jackson hits Pope's supply depot at Manassas Junction, VA.
August 29	Pope attacks Jackson at Second Bull Run (Manassas).
August 30	Longstreet reinforces Jackson; South is victorious at Second Bull Run.
September 2	McClellan replaces Pope.
September 15	Jackson victorious at Harpers Ferry, captures 12,000 Union troops.
September 17	Battle of Antietam (Sharpsburg, MD), the single bloodiest day of the war.
September 18	Lee retreats into Virginia.

September 22   Preliminary Emancipation Proclamation issued.

October 4   Maj. Gen. William S. Rosecrans defeats Confederates at Corinth, MS.

October 30   Rosecrans takes command of Union Army of the Cumberland.

November 7   Burnside takes command of Army of the Potomac, replacing McClellan.

November 21   Lee takes up defensive position at Fredericksburg, VA.

November 30   Jackson arrives at Fredericksburg.

December 11   Burnside arrives at Fredericksburg and starts to cross Rappahannock River.

December 13   Lee bests Burnside in Battle of Fredericksburg.

December 15   Army of the Potomac withdraws across the Rappahannock.

December 29   Sherman is driven back from Vicksburg, VA.

December 31   *Monitor* sinks in storm off Cape Hatteras. NC. Bragg vs. Rosecrans in heavy fighting at Murfreesboro, TN.

Facts About Key Personalities

Cited below are some of the key figures in the Civil War during the period covered by this book. Listed are their main contributions and/or their main theaters of operation. (Abbreviations used throughout are as follows: **CSA**: Confederate States of America; **USA**: United States of America.)

Anderson, Robert (1805-71): Maj. Gen. USA. Born Kentucky; West Point (1825); in command of Fort Sumter when Confederates attacked to start Civil War (Apr. 12, 1861); surrendered Apr. 13.

Banks, Nathaniel Prentiss (1816-94): Maj. Gen. USA. Born Massachusetts; state governor (1858-61); Army of the Potomac: Shenandoah Valley (1862); Army of Virginia: Cedar Mountain (Nov. 1862).

Barton, Clara (Clarissa Harlowe) (1821–1912): Born Oxford, MA.; schoolteacher; clerk in patent office, Washington, D.C.; distributed supplies and cared for the wounded during Civil War; American Red Cross founder and first president (1882–1904).

Beauregard, Pierre Gustave Toutant (1818–93): Brig. Gen. CSA. Born near New Orleans, LA.; West Point (1838); received surrender of Fort Sumter; field command First Bull Run; Army of Mississippi commander: Shiloh (1862).

Buckner, Simon Bolivar (1823–1914): Lt. Gen. CSA. Born Kentucky; West Point (1844); surrendered Fort Donelson to Grant (1862).

Buell, Don Carlos (1818–98): Maj. Gen. USA. Dept. of Ohio commander (1861); Army of Ohio commander: Shiloh.

Burnside, Ambrose E. (1824–81): Maj. Gen. USA. Born Indiana; West Point (1847); First Bull Run, Antietam; Army of Potomac commander (1862); defeated at Fredericksburg; relieved of command (1863); noted for side whiskers known as "sideburns."

Butler, Benjamin F. (1818–93): Maj. Gen. USA. Born New Hampshire. Land forces commander in capture of New Orleans (1862); military administration of the city brought cries of protest and corruption.

Davis, Jefferson (1808–89). President CSA. Born Kentucky; West Point (1828); U.S. senator from Mississippi (1847–51); 1857-61); resigned when state secedes; chosen as president of the Confederacy (1861); elected for 6 years (1862).

Grant, Ulysses S. (1822–85): Gen. USA, 18th U.S. President. Born Ohio; West Point (1843); Fort Donelson; Shiloh; commander Dept. of the Tennessee (1862).

Halleck, Henry W. (1815–72): Maj. Gen. USA. Born Westerville, NY; West Point (1839). Dept. of Missouri commander (1861–62); general in chief (1862–64).

Heintzelman, Samuel P. (1805–80): Maj. Gen. USA. First and Second Bull Run, Peninsula Campaign.

Hill, Ambrose Powell (1825–65): Lt. Gen. CSA. Born Virginia; West Point (1847); Army of Northern Virginia division: Peninsula, Bull Run, Antietam, Fredericksburg.

Hood, John Bell (1831–79): Brig. Gen. CSA. Born Kentucky; West Point (1853); Army of Northern Virginia brigade/division: Peninsula, Bull Run, Antietam, Fredericksburg.

Hooker, Joseph (1814–79): Maj. Gen. USA. Born Massachusetts; West Point (1837); called "Fighting Joe" ; Williamsburg; wounded at Antietam.

Jackson, Thomas J. "Stonewall" (1824–63): Maj. Gen. CSA. Born Virginia (now W. Va.); West Point (1846); earned nickname at First Bull Run; commander Shenandoah Valley; Army of Northern Virginia division: Peninsula, Bull Run, Antietam, Fredericksburg.

Johnston, Albert Sidney (1803–62): Gen. CSA. Born Kentucky; West Point (1826); surprised Grant at Shiloh but died in battle.

Johnston, Joseph E. (1807–91): Gen. CSA. Born Virginia; West Point (1829); First Bull Run, Fair Oaks.

Lee, Robert E. (1807–70): Gen. CSA. Born Virginia; West Point (1829); resigned U.S. Army to command Virginia troops (1861); Dept. of South Carolina, Georgia, and Florida commander (1866–62); military adviser to Davis (1862); Army of Northern Virginia commander (1862–65): Peninsula, Antietam, Fredericksburg.

Lincoln, Abraham (1809–65): 16th U.S. President. Born Kentucky; elected 1860; ordered reinforcements to Sumter (1861); called for volunteers; issued Emancipation Proclamation.

Longstreet, James (1821–1904): Lt. Gen. CSA. Born South Carolina; West Point (1842); First Bull Run; Army of Northern Virginia division: Peninsula, Second Bull Run, Antietam, Fredericksburg.

McClellan, George B. (1826–85): Maj. Gen. USA. Born Pennsylvania; West Point (1846); general in chief (1861–62); Army of the Potomac commander: Peninsula, Antietam. Replaced by Burnside (1862).

McDowell, Irvin (1818–85): Brig. Gen. USA. Born Ohio; West Point (1838); First Bull Run commander, replaced by McClellan; relieved of command after Second Bull Run.

Magruder, John B. (1810–71): Maj. Gen. CSA. Born Virginia; West Point (1830); commander Big Bethel; Army of Northern Virginia: Peninsula.

Mason, James Murray (1798–1871): Confederate diplomat. Born Virginia; Confederate commissioner to Great Britain and France. Seized on board *Trent* with Slidell (1861), imprisoned in Boston, released (1862).

Pope, John (1822–92): Maj. Gen. USA. Born Kentucky; West Point (1842); Army of the Mississippi commander; Army of Virginia commander: Second Bull Run, blamed defeat on Porter.

Porter, Fitz–John (1822–1901): Maj. Gen. USA. Born New Hampshire; West Point (1843); Shenandoah Valley, Peninsula, Second Bull Run, accused by Pope of failing to carry out orders; court-martialed, exonerated years later.

Rosecrans, William S. (1819–98): Maj. Gen. USA. Born Ohio; West Point (1842); Army of the Mississippi, succeeded Pope.

Scott, Winfield (1786–1866): Born Virginia; general in chief USA (1841–61); succeeded by McClellan.

Sherman, William T. (1820–91): Maj. Gen. USA. Born Ohio; West Point (1840); First Bull Run, Shiloh.

Slidell, John (1793–1871): Confederate diplomat. Born New York; named Confederate commissioner to France; captured on board *Trent* (1861), imprisoned in Boston, released (1862).

Stanton, Edwin M. (1814–69): U.S. secretary of war (1862–68).

Sumner, Edwin V. (1797–1863): Brig. Gen. USA. Born Boston; Army of the Potomac: Peninsula, Antietam, Fredericksburg.

Toombs, Robert (1810–85): Brig. Gen. CSA. Born Georgia; Confederate secretary of state (1861); Army of Northern Virginia: Peninsula, Bull Run, Antietam.

Wallace, Lewis (1827–1905): Brig. Gen. USA. Born Indiana; Fort Donelson; Army of the Tennessee: Shiloh.

Glossary

artillery   Weapons used by a military force.

bluff   As a noun, a high steep bank.

carnage   A bloody slaughter in battle.

depot   A place for storing goods or military supplies.

earthworks   An embankment or other construction made of earth.

eccentric   Not following an established pattern; a person having out-of-the ordinary mannerisms or behaviors.

enlistment   Enrollment in the armed forces.

flotilla   A navy unit of two or more squadrons of small warships.

fugitive   One who has run away, generally from the law.

homefront   Civilian activity during a war.

ironclad   During the Civil War, a ship covered with protective armor.

junction   An intersection of roads.

pension   Sum of money generally paid to a person after retiring from a job.

peninsula   Portion of land nearly surrounded by water.

predecessor   One who comes before, as Lincoln was President before Johnson.

recruitment   The act of enlisting people for the military.

rebellion   Opposition, generally open and sometimes armed, to a position of authority.

regiment   Military unit usually consisting of a number of battalions, which are generally composed of companies, batteries, or other units.

skirmish   Brief minor military fight.

trauma   Disordered state of mind or being, usually as result of severe injury or shock.

Bibliography

Bradford, Ned. *Battles and Leaders of the Civil War.* New York: Appleton, 1956.

Catton, Bruce. *The American Heritage New History of the Civil War.* New York: Viking, 1996.

Commager, Henry Steele. *The Blue and the Gray.* New York: Bobbs-Merrill, 1950.

Davis, William C., ed. *The Civil War.* Alexandria, VA: Time-Life Books, 1983, 28 volumes.

McPherson, James M. *For Cause & Comrades: Why Men Fought in the Civil War.* New York: Oxford Univ. Press, 1997.

Meltzer, Milton. *Voices From the Civil War.* New York: Crowell, 1989.

Ward, Geoffrey C. T*he Civil War: An Illustrated History.* New York: Knopf, 1990.

Further Reading

Blashfield, Jean F. *Mines and Minié Balls: Weapons of the Civil War.* Danbury, CT: Franklin Watts, 1997.

Bolotin, Norman and Angela Herb. *For Home and Country: A Civil War Scrapbook.* New York: Lodestar/Penguin, 1995.

Damon, Duane. *When this Cruel War Is Over: The Civil War Home Front* (People's History series). Minneapolis: Lerner, 1996.

Dear Sister: The Civil War Letters of the Brothers Gould. Compiled by Robert F. Harris and John Niflot. Westport, CT: Praeger, 1998.

Emert, Phyllis R. (Introduction). *Women in the Civil War: Warriors, Patriots, Nurses and Spies* (Perspectives on History series). Carlisle, MA: Discovery Enterprises, 1994.

Horwitz, Tony. *Confederates in the Attic: Dispatches from the Unfinished Civil War.* New York: Pantheon, 1998.

Marrin, Albert. *Commander in Chief Abraham Lincoln and the Civil War.* New York: NAL-Dutton, 1995.

Reger, James P. *The Battle of Antietam* (Battles of the Civil War series). San Diego: Lucent, 1996.

Sullivan, George. *Matthew Brady: His Life and Photographs.* New York: Dutton, 1994.

Voices of the Civil War: The Peninsula. Alexandria, VA: Time-Life, 1997.

War Between Brothers. Alexandria, VA: Time-Life, 1996.

Websites

Here are a few suggested websites with information relevant to the contents of this book. The authors and the editors take no responsibility for the accuracy of any information found on the Internet. Nor can we guarantee the availability of any website.

Abraham Lincoln Online
Everything about Honest Abe, from speeches to photographs and a Quiz of the Month. You can even join an online discussion.
http://www.netins.net/showcase/creative/lincoln.html

American Civil War Texts
Electronic texts made available by the University of Virginia.
http://etext.lib.virginia.edu/subjects/civilwar.html

Civil War Information, Documents and Archive
Large archive of primary sources and links to material on the Web.
http://users.iamdigex.net/bdboyle/cw.html

Civil War Soldiers & Sailors System
A database of 235,000 searchable records for soldiers serving in the United States Colored Troops during the Civil War.
http://www.itd.nps.gov/cwss/

Jews in the Civil War
Photographs, letters, and essays recounting the history of Jews fighting in the Civil War.
http://www.jewish-history.com/jewish.htm

Valley of the Shadow—Two Communities in the American Civil War
Online exhibition from the University of Virginia.
http://jefferson.village.virginia.edu/vshadow2/

Zoom In on the Civil War
Exploring history through artifacts.
http://www.ilt.columbia.edu/k12/history/gb/civilhome.html

Index

Note: Page numbers in italics indicate illustrations or maps.

Index

Index

Index

Acknowledgments

Cover: The Granger Collection; p.3 Brown Brothers; p.7 CORBIS/Bettmann; p.8 Museum of the City of New York; p.9 CORBIS/Bettmann ; p.10 CORBIS/Medford Historical Society Collection; pp.11, 12 CORBIS; p.14 CORBIS/Museum of the City of New York; p.17 The Granger Collection; p.18 CORBIS/The National Archives; p.20 West Point Museum Collections, United States Military Academy; p.21 The Granger Collection; p.22 National Archives; p.23 The Center for American History; p.26 CORBIS/Bettmann; pp.28, 29 CORBIS; p.31 CORBIS/Bettmann; p.32 CORBIS/Francis G. Mayer; p.33 CORBIS/Digital Stock; p.34a Chicago Historical Society; ICHI-10484; J.W. Cumberland, Army Photographer; p.34b The Granger Collection; p.35 CORBIS; p.38 The Granger Collection; p.39 CORBIS; p.42 The Granger Collection; p.45 CORBIS; p.50 CORBIS/Medford Historical Society Collection; p.51 CORBIS/Digital Stock; p.54 The Granger Collection; p.56 Courtesy Vermont Historical Society; p.59 CORBIS; p.62 CORBIS/Medford Historical Society Collection; p.63 CORBIS/Digital Stock; p.64 CORBIS/Bettmann; p.67 The Granger Collection; pp.72, 73 CORBIS; p.74 Brown Brothers; p.75 CORBIS/Bettmann; p.76 CORBIS/Digital Stock; p.77 CORBIS; p.80 Archive Photos; p.82a CORBIS/Medford Historical Society Collection; pp.82b, 83 CORBIS; p.85 Hulton Getty Images/Liaison Agency, Inc.; p.87 CORBIS; p.88 National Archives.

Map design & production: Tina Graziano, MapQuest.com